MEN AND FRIENDSHIP

BOOKS BY STUART MILLER

The Picaresque Novel

Measure, Number and Weight

Hot Springs:
*The True Adventures of the First
New York Jewish Literary Intellectual
in the Human Potential Movement*

Dimensions of Humanistic Medicine

Understanding Europeans

MEN
AND
FRIENDSHIP

STUART MILLER

JEREMY P. TARCHER, INC.
Los Angeles

Printed in the United States of America

S   10   9   8   7   6   5   4   3   2   1

For Irving, Antony, Jacqueline,
and for All True Friends

Thy friend, which is as thy own soul.
— Deuteronomy

Acknowledgments

My thanks, first, to the many hundreds of men and women in America and Europe who agreed to be interviewed about a crucial but elusive subject. Because I promised them anonymity, I have changed incidental details of their presentation in the text and cannot acknowledge them more openly here. But they have my enduring gratitude. I also want to thank a number of experts in a variety of fields who gave me bibliographical and other forms of research guidance, especially Professors James Birren, Andrew Bongiorno, Margaret Clark, Lambros Couloubaritsis, Carl Degler, Marjorie Fiske, David Forrest, Daniel Levinson, Rollo May, Thomas McFarland, Susan Merrill, Donato Morelli, Edgar Morin, Charles Muscatine, Peter Newton, William Ouchi, Letitia Anne Peplau, Eugene Simeon, Henry Nash Smith, Jacques Sojer, Frederic Speigelberg, Gerald Talley, Lawrence Weiss, John Whiting, and Vladimir Yankelevitch.

Special thanks are due to Bill Bridges, Patricia Cooper, Edith de Born, Ann Dilworth, Robert Ellis, Piero Ferrucci, Gary Friedman, Ann and Dick Grossman, Françoise Herbay, Fred Hill, Lygia Johnson, John Levy, Sterling Lord, Patricia McCall, Michael and Dulce Murphy, Sally and Seymour Peretz, Peter Solar, Joy Sweet, and Signe Warner. All gave timely support, careful criticism, and good advice. Anita McClellan, my editor at Houghton Mifflin, was essential: she believed in the book and helped it find a more perfect expression. I know that despite all this help, the book still has flaws, but they are mine alone.

Contents

Preface

Most men, particularly if they think about it, if they let themselves feel their personal truth about it, will admit they are disappointed in their friendships with other men. Men may have wives, they may even have women friends, but their relationships with other men, which could be a true echo of their own manhood, are generally characterized by thinness, insincerity, and even chronic wariness. Since most men don't let themselves think or feel about friendship, this immense collective and personal disappointment is usually concealed, sloughed over, shrugged away.

Over the years, the pain of men's loneliness, the weakening of their male ties, the gradually accumulating disillusionment with male friends, the guilt at their own betrayals of others, are just ignored. Partly it is a result of resignation. We lower our expectations. The older we get the more we accept our essential friendlessness with men. Of course, men remember another time when they were much younger, when they believed in true friendship, when they thought they had it, when they raised imaginary boyish swords to the musketeers' promise: "All for one and one for all!" When they had, perhaps as late as college, at least one other man with whom they were deeply connected. With a smile, we all remember.

Childish things to be put away, we say to ourselves, though all men secretly cherish the memories. Our lives go forward — racing to keep pace, to get ahead, to pay the bills, to take care of children and wives, to survive and prosper.

There may come a moment of crisis — divorce, when coupled friends are suddenly no longer very interested; the loss of a job or career, when formerly chummy colleagues suddenly don't remember to call; or, less dramatically, a moment in middle life when ordinary companionships suddenly seem empty, insufficient. In such circumstances, certain men may feel moved to search for male friendship. Very rarely, one of them actually finds a true friend.

This book is about the seeking of such a renewal: a search for true friendship between adult men. It is partially based on nearly a thousand interviews with men who live in the heart of our modern, post-industrial society: businessmen and lawyers, psychologists and physicians, government employees, editors, artists and writers, sociologists and philosophers, physicists, journalists, and many others. These interviews took place in many parts of the United States and Europe. However, the resulting book is not sociology; it is not science.

Besides using interviews, the book is based on extensive reading about friendship, not just in the classics — Montaigne and Cicero, Aristotle and Plato — but also in psychology and anthropology and in contemporary research about modern friendship. However, the book is not a report on the philosophical writings on friendship or on the writings of any academic discipline.

My method is warmer and less systematic, more inward and intimate than that of these other authors. I could find no other way to get at the truth about friendship between men. Nearly every abstract treatise written about friendship, including some of the ancient classics and nearly all of the modern scientific and popular books, is cold. The books leave out the emotional realities. The vast majority of my interviews were in many ways the same. Men will often glow when one brings up the topic of friendship. They are visibly glad to contemplate the subject and to discuss it. But, in general, they won't really show or tell you much about what friendship means to them. This is a common exchange:

Q. Do you have friends?
A. A few.
Q. Tell me about them.
A. There's really not much to tell.
Q. Why do you like them?
A. Well, they're nice, we have fun together, share interests.
Q. Are they important to you?
A. Sure.

And so forth.

Most people find the subject unutterable. Some will, of course, talk popular sociology, others will discover philosophical truisms, but they can't really talk about friendship itself. Partly, it is a lack of poetry in most men. They do not have the words for such a subject. Partly, it is a taboo against looking at something so sacred. Often, it is a reluctance to look at something so painful.

I came to realize that if I were to try to stay close to the core of my subject, I would have to get involved as more than author.

This is accordingly, a bicameral book. On the one hand, it is a report about the state of male friendship in the modern world. On the other hand, it records parts of my personal journey into the depths of male friendship.

. . .

My quest for deeper male friendships began before it occurred to me to write for others about the subject. I kept a journal of my own experiences and what they meant to me. Gradually, I was moved to keep copies of my letters to friends and their letters to me. I wanted to serve my own quest; to understand in detail the blockages and obstacles; to chart the microcontours of experience

from which male friendship is constructed; to register the unre-
membered acts of kindness and of love, the little daily risks, even
the forgotten or squelched moments of rage or disappointment at
a telephone call not returned. Occasionally I felt there was something monstrous about such self-consciousness. Especially today,
friendship is supposedly a relationship one gets or doesn't get,
takes or leaves, lightly and without much self-awareness or concern. However, I had decided to take friendship between men
seriously, and my daemon drove me on. I was brought to realize
that some of this personal material needed to find a place in the
book I had determined to write.

Rather than reduce the interviews to statistical averages or to
summarize them abstractly, I came to see the necessity of present-
ing the most telling ones whole, often with the scene evoked and
my own reactions. Sometimes the journal excerpts and interviews
contain their own analysis; at other times I discuss their more
general meanings from a later, detached perspective. In certain
cases, no abstract analysis can exhaust the meaning of the journal
excerpts. Particulary with these, but also with all the lived material,
the reader must examine his own experience of male friendship, his
own feelings, and find his own significance. I ask you to follow me
then, not only into the occasional records of my own discoveries,
but more important, into discoveries of your own.

I have been fortunate in being able to pursue this subject with
enormous focus. Over three years I was gradually to give male
friendship one of the primary places in my life. All this exploring,
outer and inner, is intended to serve the reader. But one caveat:
though in some of its aspects this is a personal book, it is not
autobiography. Because the subject is the search for true male
friendship, I do not discuss my work or marriage in any detail.

Early in my quest for male friendship, my own life was in
considerable disorder. Call it a midlife crisis. A recent painful divorce, career uncertainties, the first health problems of middle age,
were upon me, and all these circumstances impelled me to reach

out to others, to examine the relative superficiality of cordial relations with former male colleagues and old acquaintances, the network that most men — as long as all goes well in their lives — easily refer to as friends.

Certain passages of the journal reflect this background of turmoil. Rather than whitewash them, I have let them stand. Without such a crisis, I might never have started my search for male friendship or eventually gotten the idea to write about it. Most of us encounter difficulties at one time or another and that is part of friendship. Not only must we deal with the effects on our friends, we must deal with the pain when our needs aren't met in a society where friendship is not deeply honored.

Two years into the quest, my own life had partly reconstituted itself; I had remarried. Then, a year's stay in Europe gave me more time to work on the book and to focus more deeply on the need for friendship. Finally, I returned to America to gather the results of this careful attention.

Though not all men have crises at midlife, and very few think of writing a book about the search for friendship or plunge themselves into the relative isolation of a foreign culture, I believe that the inner experiences of friendship I describe in these special outer circumstances have a broad typicality. Without the special conditions, I might have remained less conscious, and some of the truth about male friendship might not have emerged.

The scope of the book had to be finite. Various social groups, not just in America but also abroad, have not been investigated, nor has every possible profession. Nor have friendships between men and women received all the attention that subject deserves. I have had to eschew these and other interesting topics because I was pressed by my own and a collective question. Can adult men — men in their thirties and older, most married or otherwise coupled and busy at careers; men in the mainstream of modern urban life — find the comradeship, the succor, the joy and devotion of true friendship with at least one man?

1

True Friendship
Between Men

The first time I went out interviewing and told someone I was thinking of writing a book on male friendship, it was a sunny spring day in California. I had been divorced for a year and had already started trying to deepen my existing friendships. But it was only recently that the idea to write a book on the subject had occurred to me.

The person I chose was a reliable sort: career man, married, grown children, grandchildren. For a long time he had been head of a humanities department at a university. I respected him. We had first met, years before, because he had defied the university authorities: while not very political himself, he believed in civil liberties and would have resigned, if necessary, to protect those of his students. Indeed, he had been a sort of mentor for me in my youthful days as a professor. So, he was not a friend, because friendship is a more equal relationship, but still someone with whom I felt a personal connection.

Though he had been a teacher for forty-five years before he had retired, gnarled and thin, his western origins still showed through. He was, if you will, the cowboy-scholar, and I watched him stretch one long leg over another as he leaned back in his chair, his hands clasped behind his bald head. He had the assurance of a man who had risen to the top of his profession even when taking risks.

He squinted at me in the pained way he liked to crease his face when he wanted you to know he was thinking seriously. "Male friendship. You mean you're going to write about homosexuality? That's what everybody will think, at least. Could be dangerous for you."

I couldn't believe his reaction. Surely the great tradition of male friendship, celebrated in the West by Homer and Aristotle and Cicero, by Montaigne and Shakespeare and Pope, was what people would think of when I said "male friendship." Surely they would call to mind the expedition of Gilgamesh and Enkidu, the terrible wrath of Achilles at the slaughter of his friend Patrocles, the love of David for Jonathan, which surpassed family and political loyalties, the heroic self-sacrifice of Oliver for his friend Roland. At the very least they would think of the more recent movie images of men loyal to and caring for one another — *The Deerhunter, Butch Cassidy and the Sundance Kid,* and *Breaker Morant.*

"Mebbe," he muttered, "mebbe I'm too affected by the gay scene around here." He didn't sound convinced.

We talked. Yes, he had still a couple of friends. Didn't see them much anymore. Didn't even hear from them much. In fact, the high point, what he really remembered, was in the twenties. He had shared literary enthusiasms with his friends in the West when the only other people around were *real* cowboys. It had been a strong bond to be able to talk about Hemingway and Paris among the deer and the antelope. He smiled with fond remembrance. It was a long time ago.

I left the philosopher and walked over to the science building to see another former acquaintance, another retired professor, but this one in his small laboratory. The counter was dull black marble, the Bunsen burner long unused, the blackboard covered with calculations and mathematical symbols and the smudges, underneath those, of erased layers of thought. This man, too, had risen to the top of his profession. A renowned scholar, he was short, fat, and cheerful, whereas the first had been tall, thin, and dour.

When I explained what I was up to, he looked uncharacteristically distant as he said, "Mostly it has been death that has deprived me of my friends. You must be careful. You know, of course, that people will think you are writing about homosexuality."

"What I'm interested in is the loving relationship between adult men! Is it possible that the situation has gotten so bad that people think male friendship is something queer?"

He smiled sorrowfully.

Everywhere I have gone there has been the same misconception. The bizarre necessity to explain, at the beginning, that my subject is not homosexuality.

The fear of homosexuality and how it affects the possibilities of male friendship in our times are topics that need contemplating, and we will come back to them. The point here, however, is that the estate of male friendship — indeed, of nearly all human relationships — is sufficiently sunk that mere sex remains at the center of people's imaginations. The only moving human relationships that people seem able to conjure up are erotic ones.

It is hard to prove that adult male friendship has died, just as it is hard to prove logically that something doesn't exist: nowhere is there a purple cow. A recent survey of the readers of *Psychology Today*, purporting to be the most extensive poll of American men and women about friendship, reports that most who responded are satisfied with the quality of their friendships. They confide in their friends, tend to turn to them in times of emotional crises, and tend to find their friends more important as they all get older. The editors see such replies as tending to contradict "clichés" about the impersonality and anomie of life in modern cities. The editors note that the survey results "give cold comfort to social critics."

Perhaps. And yet in examining such a survey, one notes that the thousands of people who responded did so voluntarily. One has not yet heard from the nearly three million readers who did not respond. In addition, only a small proportion of those who replied were men, and only fifteen percent were over thirty-five years old. Perhaps the low age of the self-selected sample explains why most respondents reported their friendships had most frequently been formed in childhood. One wonders how events will look to them in a decade or more.

In fact, deep friendship between adult men is quite rare in our society. Most interesting in this regard are the findings of Professor Daniel Levinson's team of social scientists at Yale, the psychologists, sociologists, and anthropologists who patiently studied a cross section of adult American men over many years. In the book *The Seasons of a Man's Life,* they report:

> In our interviews, friendship was largely noticeable by its absence. As a tentative generalization we would say that close friendship with a man or woman is rarely experienced by American men. This is not something that can be adequately determined by a questionnaire or mass survey. The distinction between friend and acquaintance is often blurred. A man may have a wide social network in which he has amicable, "friendly" relationships with many men and perhaps a few women. In general, however, most men do not have an intimate male friend of the kind that they recall fondly from boyhood or youth.

Here we get further toward a definition of real male friendship: "the kind" that men "recall fondly from boyhood or youth."

I have found that friendship, especially adult male friendship, is something impossible to describe in the analytical terms that scientific writers will muster about the subject: "male bonding," "trust," "intimacy," "sharing," "confidant," "helper." The reality defies all such categories as it eludes, also, "loyalty," "warmth," "affection," "supportiveness," "common interests," and "common activities." And as it eludes "acceptance" and "self-disclosure" and even "presence."

Nevertheless, all these expressions help to evoke, to materialize out of a cloud of abstraction, that subtle reality of which we speak. We can partially evoke it by its negation. This is a matter of tone of voice. A widow, seventy-two years old, recalls: "My husband had a very big funeral. My family was surprised and pleased, despite our pain, at how many came. Over three hundred people. There were the couples we had seen all through the years. There were people he knew from his jobs, and a sprinkling of relatives. The majority were men.

"And yet, when I think back upon that terrible time, and upon his good life, which had more meaning and color than most, I can't say that my husband really had any friends. Odd, isn't it, for such a busy man? One who was so very well liked?"

• • •

As my early interviewing went on, there was reason to think that American men no longer know what a friend is. If I simply asked them about their friendships, often they told me everything was fine. Sure, they see people, to a degree confide in people, to a degree trust people. They have, as the Yale study suggests, a network of relationships. They are not anchorites. But as the psychologist Abraham Maslow put it, that doesn't mean men have a friend in the world.

I talked at length to a man I know who is in his fifties, divorced, and attractive — not just attractive to women, but to people in general. He is at the center of a vast professional and social network of contacts. An administrator of a humanitarian institute, he is constantly trying to help others. So he introduces Bill to Joe, in the hope they will collaborate on a book. And he introduces Arthur to Harry, hoping they will launch a project in Africa. As time goes on, these people tend to see each other — first at work, then after work, and they become one another's society. The man who started it all is pleased, and he is the beneficiary of more and more such successful pairings. He has lunch or dinner with a "friend" virtually every afternoon and night. Because he has introduced so many people to one another, these luncheons and dinners are increasingly filled with talk of those mutually related individuals. This man, more than many people in our society, seems to live supported by a virtual web of love, one that reaches fifty miles in every direction and is constantly being reinforced with new knots of meetings and pleasant exchanges.

"I was very sick the other night," he said to me, stirring sugar into his coffee. Indeed, he looked a little paler than usual and his big shoulders seemed to slump. "I was in my office, a little after five, on Friday, after everyone else had gone home. And I just fell down. I was hot. Then cold. And my stomach was all knotted up. I could hardly move."

"Were you conscious?"

"Yes, though mostly of pain."

"Did you call someone."

"No."

"Well, what did you do? You should have called someone."

"I was very afraid, of course. But I waited. And then, crawling, I made it down the stairs. And somehow, even though it was dark as hell out and raining, I managed to get into the car and to drive home. I've never been so sick in my life. Really, I thought I might die."

"You should have called someone. Why didn't you call me or one of your other friends?"

"I don't know. I just didn't. And, anyway, it went away the next day."

"If anything like this ever happens again you must call me. Please." I tried to get him to look me in the eye and say yes.

"Sure," he said, but I didn't believe him.

How odd that when the crunch comes, he will not call. Does this man have a friend?

• • •

Because many Americans talk so easily about their friendships, social critics like to call us back to order. Novelists, for example, force us to contemplate the traditional definitions of friendship and to measure our relationships against them. Take the following conversation, in Joseph Heller's *Good as Gold*, between men who have known each other for twenty years and who are presently working together at the highest levels of our government:

> "I suppose you're right, Ralph. The important thing is not our social worlds but our friendship. There's a definition of a friend I once heard expressed by my Swedish publisher. He's Jewish, Ralph, and he lived in Germany under Hitler as a child until his family escaped. He has only one test of a friend now, he told me. 'Would he hide me?' is the question he asks. It's pretty much my test of a friend too, when I come down to it. Ralph, if Hitler returns, would you hide me?'
>
> The question threw Ralph into a flurry . . . "Oh, gosh, Bruce," he exclaimed hastily, "we're not friends . . ."
>
> Gold felt this more than he wished to show. "You used my work at school, Ralph. We were pretty close then."
>
> "That was college, Bruce," said Ralph, "and it was important that I get my degree. But this is only government. People in government don't have friends, Bruce, just interests and ambitions."

Do you love your friend enought to put your life in danger? It is the kind of question that quickly puts facile talk about having friends in perspective.

Useful as Heller's query is, to my mind, it is not, in itself, a total definition of friendship between men. There's a good chance that the people who might actually save you from Nazis and other assorted monsters might not be friends at all but just plain decent folk. Moreover, the definition posed by the question is simply too behavioral. There is a tendency to define friends merely in terms of action: How often do you *see* them? Would they *help* you? Can you *confide* in them? All important questions. But friendship often does not involve gross behaviors at all. It is, rather, something subtle and inward, a series of inner movements and responses.

Let us try another question, then.

You are an adult American male, somewhere past thirty. It is night. You have gotten into bed. With the deliberation that comes at a certain age you close your eyes. You have long since ceased to be sure that they will close by themselves. Now the mind begins its own regular routines: sorting and filing and inventorying your recent experience. What were yesterday's tasks? What will be to-morrow's obligations? Are you up to them? Does your wife still love you? Are the children going to be all right?

As you lie there, waiting for inner quiet, reviewing the day, thinking about tomorrow, wife, child, do you also habitually think about your friend? Do you think with what delight you will see him tomorrow? With what disappointment you won't see him? Do you wonder how he will straighten out *his* family's problems?

When one has a really close friend, his image is part of the carousel of vehicles and beasts that appears at the entrance to one's personal underworld. Like Ulysses, you look forward to seeing the great Achilles that you knew. If at such junctures in life as the space between consciousness and sleep your friend is with you, in your imagination, then you have a friend. If not, if a friend is seldom there, then it doesn't matter how many favors people will do for you, how many rounds of golf you play with them, how much you help one another in your work.

Shakespeare has the phrase for this critical dimension of friendship. As Hamlet is dying, he begs Horatio to live on: "If thou didst ever hold me in thy heart, / Absent thee from felicity a while / And ... draw thy breath in pain / To tell my story." As much as anything else, friendship is the inner habit of holding someone who is neither spouse nor relative, nor teacher, nor lover, in your heart.

Notice here that we are not talking about men in groups; friendship is more selective and personal, almost always two by two. And we are not talking about those exciting, sometimes profound, but necessarily transitory relationships that feed off a particular social context: comrades in the same political or religious debates and struggles, co-ideologues, teammates, nor even those bonds formed by living through dangerous situations together. Many people believe that men in hazardous occupations have friends, but usually, when the danger passes, so does the active being of friendship; it is replaced by a warm shared nostalgia. True, friendship may sometimes arise in all such contexts, but it is finally independent of them. Friendship is its own context.

• • •

There are particular experiences when friends are together — perhaps as varied in their details as the number of men who can make friendships — that also help define the essence of the relationship. I talked to a man in his fifties who has had his ups and downs in the world, a writer whose work is marked by its terrifying excursions into the darker sides of existence: a terrible pain to being human. This man, with a face roughly torn by lines of care, has his own experience of friendship. Explaining how with age friendship has become rarer and rarer in his life, he says:

I think people who develop a real friendship are men who have been very badly hurt and unconsciously go to that most exact of human places to heal themselves. In some complicated way, friendship at its most perfect is related to deep suffering and deep illness; the acute horror of being forced into desolation by a society that clearly has little real interest in human values. So when people go toward each other and love one another, there's a kind of deep, deep medication. Real friendship, then, is a kind of divine act that enables two people to share feelings, to have feelings that life denies continually. It's a way of outsmarting life, which is continually getting at you anyway, no matter how rich or smart you are . . . It's the one chance you have of getting on top of it. It requires all your belief in the possibility that you can walk on water with somebody because of the sheer electrical discharge of love. It's a kind of hydrojet you're on.

A younger but also middle-aged man, a stout psychotherapist with many children, describes the moment of friendship:

A deep and powerful, soft and relaxed quality of simply breathing together. And strong moments when one's brain is rapaciously excited around an idea that you're sharing. A visceral intimacy, sort of like eating a wonderful meal together. To eat, to be filled, no competition; just a kind of gustatory, visceral, endomorphic filling. Very soft. Two comrades sitting at the edge of a rock looking at the ocean, or going for a wonderful, easy stroll through a city. There is no sense of danger, distrust, threat. The only thing that one is on guard about, if at all, is not to say something that will hurt, should it come up.

Such descriptions help us recall the experience of friendship and remind us of its rarity. But there remains the further question: What is the particular note of maleness in experiences of friendship? Many people, in our liberated age especially, maintain that there is no reality to the idea of male friendship as distinct from a friendship between the sexes or between women. But though the male element in male friendship must ultimately remain a mystery, we can suggest some of its aspects.

There is a particular background to the intimacy one experiences with a close male friend: the usual rivalry and struggle of man against man. In modern competitive society, all men to some extent are seen as potential enemies. In school they are competitors. On the playing field they are competitors. After school hours they are potential aggressors. As we grow to adulthood, they confront us with their criticisms, with their maneuvering for positions in the hierarchies of power, money, celebrity, accomplishment, and the conquest of women. In the bureaucracies within which most of us work, men lie in wait, perhaps to help, perhaps to betray and take our places. In the bureaucracies we deal with — to get our taxes paid, our cars registered, our health care delivered — the strange man can look upon us as an object, as a nuisance, as a potential wrongdoer. On the road, in the heavy steel armor of his automobile, the other man is ever ready to overtake, to pass, to cut off. We live our lives in a world of alien, seemingly tame but, we know, potentially dangerous males.

Most of the time we ignore the danger; we smile and stay cheerful, we coyly make gestures of submission or brave our way, we keep our sense of humor, we get by. But one measure of our deep habitual tension is the special relaxation and easiness we feel with a male friend. These are different from the deep comfort a woman lover can give, though all the world's instruments attached to brain and heart would have a hard time measuring the difference. With a male friend, we experience a serene excitement, a softening that thaws the shoulders.

Attending to such sensations, we can think that Wilhelm Reich was not so crazy when he talked about male "body armor." He described how the pliant bodies of male children gradually harden into heavy layers of tissue, adult breastplates, a deep and permanent tightness and tension of neck and gut and thigh, even when the man doesn't exercise. With a real man friend, for some moments, this tight armoring melts. One breathes more slowly and deeply. The back relaxes, and in minute ways even the testicles relax. Safety. The safety that comes from experiencing in an unmediated way that this man among men will not threaten. And that this man will, quite literally, protect your ass, as you will his should other men strike.

Usually, these are unconscious sensations and feelings, but they are nevertheless experienced. A psychologist in his sixties who has an extremely deep relationship with both his wife and one special man friend, has grappled with the notion and come up with this evocative distinction: "With Cynthia, I think, 'She will stand by me in everything, shoulder to shoulder,' but with Michael, I think, 'Back to back — he will help me fight back to back.'"

A tough army colonel tells me, "You know how often, in the most peaceful times and places, you pick a restaurant seat with your back against the wall and facing the door? It's instinctive, unconscious, primitive. And it's not only soldiers who do it — I've noticed it in stockbrokers, lawyers, lots of people. I think one aspect of male friendship is the sense that your back will be covered."

There are other ways to describe the masculine dimensions of friendship. To trust another man fully is to experience the pleasure of moving from expectations of roughness to those of softness and peace. Ordinarily, when we moderns think of other men physically, they are but shaggy creatures to us — rough beards and tough skin — not at all like the women we long to touch. Indeed, the physical attraction women feel for other men baffles us. We shrink from the adult physique of other men the way we often shrink from our own. As the poet Delmore Schwartz put it, we are disgusted with "the heavy bear that goes with me, a manifold honey to smear his face." In deep friendship this cultivated aversion and alienation from masculinity, inevitably including a degree of self-alienation, is from moment to moment forgone.

It is not that friends necessarily ever touch. Rather that in friendship we are curiously drawn by the other man's inner beauty past the reflexive aversion to his outer appearance. We are drawn by his wit, the set of his eyes that makes us think we are seen. We are drawn by his apparent gentleness, his directness, his valor. We are drawn by his energy, a male force we share and that reinforces ours just when the world and time seem to have flattened us out altogether. Past the shaggy-beast exterior, the threatening otherness that is also our own physical self, we find a heart that beats with ours, a brain that chimes with ours, an understanding that includes the same masculinity that is, too often, a burden in this life.

A middle-aged police detective hints at the depths of this secret knowledge. "One of the recognitions I share with my present-day friends is that we all have the initiation of maturity. We've had to do certain things to be independent and we know what they are. The shameful ones, the worthy ones, and the breaking of our illusions. You recognize that in the other man, it never has to be spoken, and you build on that."

An aspect of the pleasurable essence of male friendship, then, consists in an imaginative going forth toward and beyond the perpetual threat of combat. It is to enter the shared knowledge of battles lost and won with caring and simple acceptance of mutual maleness.

This experience of generic wariness and repulsion yielding to taking a risk and then to being together is repeated over and over in any real friendship. When it happens, we feel known. Even the beast that is our mutual fate is known. And in some curious way, together we redeem the beast, and we can shout and dance — or we could, if such rejoicings were permitted in our world — with satisfaction at being men.

Then, for no deeper reason than the transient quality of all human satisfaction, the experience is lost and one is again isolated, facing another alien man.

This process is nothing exotic; at a certain level of intensity, it can happen in the most ordinary settings and with men who are only casual friends. You have come early to the restaurant where a friend is to meet you for lunch. You sit at the cloth-covered table playing with the silverware. There is a stir in the distance and you raise your eyes. A man approaches. For the instant it seems just another male shape. You keep your armor on. As he comes closer, you see it is your friend, but you are not sure whether he is in a good mood or not. The armor stays on. You smile, you get out of your chair, you hold out the hand to grab the hand, you keep scanning, discreetly, to see if it's all right. Maybe, now, you'll take your armor off, let it melt away, some or all. Or maybe you'll just keep smiling and busy yourself with "Hello, how are you, how much time will you have, we'd better order, the salmon looks good . . ." Until it fits — if it does, somehow, maybe after a couple of drinks — and by some imperceptible process you are together. But then, during the meal, you may stiffen again, inwardly, at something he said, or you thought he said, and you will reach out imaginary stiff arms to put him off. At the end, when he hurries away as you do, you will with the slightest hidden bitterness forsake him because he forsook you or, in any case, you've got to be a real man, tough and ready, again. Lunch is over. The talk is over The game is finished.

The experience of meeting another man on that safe inner ground is so special and so important that men will go through rather strange antics to have it. Many commentators have decried the fact that American men, particularly, seem to have to act tough with one another. They have criticized the poking, the proverbial back-slapping, the ironic joking, and the near fighting that men use in approaching one another.

We are all familiar with that rude striking and provoking, even though it is now passing out of fashion. But what is it for? Is it simply a denial of tenderness, a masking of gentler feelings? It is that and also, paradoxically, its opposite. In our culture, where expressing the kinder feelings between adult males is simply not usual, some men evoke those feelings by mock denial. It amounts to a dramatization, almost a parody, of the usual combative relationship between competitive men that can yield itself to real contact.

Joseph Heller reports that he never says sentimental things to his closest friends; for example, that he cares for them. Men don't do that, he insists; it wouldn't seem right. Rather, he makes fun of them. When his friend Mel Brooks interviews him for an article and goes off into a long question in which Brooks is obviously struggling to form his ideas, Heller says, "Oh, but no one cares what *you* think, Mel."

Heller's is a mock assault. It is not intended to hurt. The shock is received as a sting, like the proverbial clap on the back, and a feeling of intimacy and relaxedness is evoked by a kind of magnetic attraction of the opposite. We don't *really* fight, we are really friends. Of course. After much such mutual thumping, softened with enough alcohol, men of this sort will eventually get down to the warmer feelings they cannot easily express. There are even some men who will simply not trust you until they have physically or otherwise fought with you. They must emphasize the armor, use it, before they can allow themselves to put it aside. The famous wrestling scene in D. H. Lawrence's *Women in Love* is of this kind.

There are other aspects of the masculine expression of friendship — tendencies toward mutual action or wildness, for example — that are often frustrated by too highly organized a society. One that seems especially important is the admiration close men friends feel for each other. While most of modern life demands that we be ready to compete (thereby ever-honing us to belittle, to criticize, to search for flaws), friendship allows us to esteem the other freely. When men who have close friends or men who in their youth had close friends talk about them, their eyes shine, their faces light up, and they appreciate, shamelessly, the other's qualities of character, strength, courage, versatility, intelligence, humor, generosity. Such appreciation is in itself a pleasurable release to our otherwise frustrated sense of justice, expressing our best traditional ideas of manliness. More selfishly, those qualities we do admire we magically add, through the bond we feel and in our unconscious imaginations, to our own.

These are some of the special aspects of close male friendship: a willingness to take a dangerous stand for another; a special relaxation and safety; an end to competitiveness, alienation, and self-alienation; a pleasure in doing masculine justice to others, an enhancement of men's own vitality and being. Above all, a holding in the heart.

2

The Death
of Intimacy
in Our Times

Let me confess, straightaway, that an understanding of male friendship only came to me slowly and often painfully. I had begun my personal quest a full year before I had the idea to write a book on the subject and interviewed the cowboy-scholar. It took the better part of the second year before I had a relatively clear sense of what I was personally seeking.

During these first two years, I pursued my personal search for deeper friendships with old acquaintances as well as with a few new men. At the same time, and partly because of the personal search, I found myself forced to deal with impersonal questions. In looking for better relationships I ran up against many mysterious obstacles. The quest was frequently so difficult that sometimes I doubted the very legitimacy of the enterprise. Indeed, I often thought that there was something wrong with me for seeking what only five percent of all American men had. I worried that for a modern man I had unusual needs for intimacy.

After all, what is "a man" nowadays?

Somebody who stands alone, independent of all ties. A man is supposed to give up his callow buddies in late adolescence or in his twenties, to get a job, to get married, to get serious. If something seems missing in his life, he is supposed to forget about it, to be stoical about his disappointments. Our society seems to say that a real man needs and wants nobody — except maybe a woman. And even she can be temporary.

Fortunately, as I entertained and suffered from such doubts, my reading and interviewing during that second year brought me a clearer sense of the historical normality of the need for close human ties as well as a clearer sense of the many reasons for male friendship's current disappearance. While these realizations did not entirely stop the pain of my self-doubt, they confirmed that needs for intimacy are as perennial as human culture and that the difficulties I was experiencing were, at least in part, the result of vast new social forces. The decline of friendship in our time must be seen against the decline in intensity and closeness of all human relationships.

• • •

We have forgotten how close human beings once were to one another. Intimacy, which we tend to associate simply with the relatively occasional sexual act, was in fact the normal condition of most of the human race. To think that an interest in a relationship like male friendship is something strange, connoting a lack of willingness to stand on one's own, is to deny our nature and our past. For until not very many years ago, two hundred at the very outside, one was born into intimacy, lived and worked in it, and died in it. In this sense, no one has ever been alone before now.

In certain remote parts of Europe, Roman Catholic and southern parts particularly, such historical intimacy is still lived to some extent. But the first example comes from northern England in the year 1619: the life of a typical bakery as described by the historian Peter Laslett. Thirteen people make up the staff: the baker, his wife, four paid employees called journeymen, two maid-servants, two apprentices, and the baker's three children. Everyone ate every meal together; no one went home at night; indeed, by

law, only the journeymen could live elsewhere. All were depen-
dents of the baker: all worked together, even the children, within
the household. Moreover, this was no mere commercial enterprise:
family was the only word used to describe such a group of people.
I will not sentimentalize the old ways. For the modern temper,
the notion of being locked up for life within a single family — the
same faces, one place, one metier, the lack of variety and personal
freedom — may well seem horrible. And such an arrangement
surely had its share of tyranny, exploitation, jealousy, and tension.
Life was hard then and, in general, human relations were not
characterized by tenderness nor did people always have delicate
sensibilities. But as the social historian Philippe Ariès notices,
though our ancestors lived in a kind of promiscuity, it was also an
arrangement of mutual assistance, an arrangement that did not
exclude hate, to be sure, but it was "a brand of hate that resembled
love. A life led cheek to cheek, very tight, an extremely tight
fabric."

The memory of that tightness is still in our bones. While few
of us would elect to go back to pre-industrial conditions, we feel
the loss of that intimacy even when we are taught to think that the
need for deep intimacy is something odd.

Barbara Tuchman, the author of *A Distant Mirror,* describes
another aspect of traditional Western European existence.
Medieval life was

> lived collectively in infinite numbers of groups, orders, associ-
> ations, brotherhoods. Never was man less alone. Even in bed-
> rooms married couples often slept in company with their ser-
> vants and children. Except for hermits and recluses, privacy
> was unknown. As nobles had their orders of chivalry, the
> common man had the *confrérie* or brotherhood of his trade or
> village, which surrounded him at every crux of life . . . Usually
> numbering from 20 to 100 members . . . they accompanied a
> member to the town gates when he went off on a pilgrimage

and marched in his funeral when he died. If a man was con-
demned to be executed, fellow members accompanied him to
the scaffold. If he drowned accidentally as in the case at Bor-
deaux, they searched the Garonne for three days for his body.

They staged religious plays and mounted costumed parades on
feast days. In contemporary Europe, picturesque vestiges of these
traditions are trotted out for tourists, but one can imagine the
intensity and meaningfulness of such occasions in the tightly
sealed communities of the fourteenth century. The *confréries* had
their patron saints, their rites and oaths, their deep sociability and
their frictions.

Even in the normal hierarchies of feudal relations — whether
baker to journeyman or peasant to lord — the bond between
people was not seen as primarily economic in nature. You didn't
just work for your lord, you had to fight for him and he had to
protect you. As Marx observed, economic exchange existed within
the context of personal relations.

• • •

How much intimacy we moderns have lost with particular regard
to the friendship ties between men has been brilliantly summarized
by the anthropologist Robert Brain in his important book *Friends
and Lovers*. He takes us back in cultural time, even beyond the
Western Middle Ages, to the normal conditions of older human
societies. Among the Bangwa of Africa, for example, young men
who are friends spend long hours "in each other's company, holding hands when they walk together in the market . . . As they grow
older friendships become increasingly valued — elders . . . sit
around with their friends, chatting about local politics . . . trouble
with an obstreperous young wife." In this society, a man's best
friend is trusted to the extent of sharing the same bench as his
wives, an act that if done by another would be considered adultery.
In addition, the best friend has endless obligations and duties,

from helping his friend to marry to being among the chief mourners at his funeral and defending his estate after he dies.

Such historical patterns of male friendship are nearly universal. One finds them in indigenous cultures as far apart as Africa, Polynesia, Melanesia, and South America. They are typical of humankind.

But if intimacy and friendship were the norms of human life, such relationships, which existed not only between best male friends but also between all kinds of pairs — fathers and children, husbands and wives, uncles and nieces, proprietors and workers — are remorselessly undercut by modern civilization.

Economic theoreticians like Karl Marx blame, above all, the rise of the market economy. Labor became simply an economic commodity. I buy your time. You, as an individual, are no longer the loved and resented familiar; you become an economic bundle. Your value fluctuates according to an impersonal market: your value to me, to others, to yourself. Consequently, you want to become mobile, to move quickly to where your value is highest and you can get the highest return on your labor.

The more opportunity there is to move to receive higher wages — or the greater the necessity to move when markets for labor shift — the more portable intimate life must become. The result is that the married couple or the very small family is all we can bear to take with us, and all other associations such as the extended family and friendship decline in importance.

As early as 1894, the great French sociologist Emile Durkheim saw the far-reaching effects of this new mobility, predicting that with the coming of a market economy, all the institutions that held social life together — such as the church, the family, the club or voluntary association (like the medieval *confrérie*), and the neighborhood — would decline in influence and vitality. As a result, people would lose a sense of their own identities, they would suffer from what he called anomie. Because of this lack of intimacy, Durkheim also forecast that the modern world would be visited by unprecedented plagues of divorce, mental disease, suicide, homicide, and alcohol and drug addiction. We all know how right he was.

Not only the rise of the market economy contributes to a decline in the depth and permanence of all human relationships, including men's friendships, but virtually every other tendency in modern life has the same effect. In religion, for example. The decline of medieval Roman Catholicism and the rise of Protestantism have helped dissolve the old patterns of relating. The Protestant emphasis on the individual soul — as opposed to a *relationship* between the soul and the Church and the Church and God — leaves every man on his own. And every woman, too. The whole hierarchy of spiritual entities, from human individual through priest and congregation, through Church and pope, through ascending orders of angels, all the way to the Divine, is swept away. And the individual is left to work out his salvation by himself, in solitary and naked glory (or misery), on his knees before God. It is a free, heroic role most of us want to keep, of course, but it is a prototypically lonely one. Such ways of thinking have released great energies, but they have also undermined our attachment to others and our trust in them. The desire for heroic salvation calls us back, over and over again, to our solitary selves.

Furthermore, the rise of Protestantism was gradually accompanied by the decline of Christianity, generally. This development helped take the soul out of human relationships altogether. The solitary individual is increasingly seen as having no soul himself. We look at each other, as the psychologist Rollo May has said, "with the feeling — 'He's no more than a bunch of bones and so am I.' Where is the flesh? Where is the warmth? There is a facsimile of it with men and women, though often it can be largely mechanical. But with men, this holding and sharing of warmth — all we would think to have with real friends — is mostly absent."

Along with religion, virtually all of modern philosophy declares this separation of individuals from one another. For

Gottfried Leibniz, the seventeenth-century German philosopher, for example, reality is organized into "monads," solid, impenetrable substances, and between them there are no doors or windows. Such a philosophy is in many respects positive. It explains earlier attitudes that made possible the great voyages of Magellan and Columbus, the starting out by oneself into Nothing. But since the time of Leibnitz, it is hard to find philosophers who stress relatedness in any way. There is Henri Bergson, and before him the romantics, and Marx with his talk of the brotherhood of revolution, and Martin Buber with his I and Thou, but by and large modern philosophy is about aloneness. We are forlorn, abandoned.

Social and political theory, too, especially here in the United States, emphasizes isolation rather than relationship. Alexis de Tocqueville, the nineteenth-century French historian who studied the nature of American democracy, observed that there has never been a country so committed to individual wants as opposed to collective needs. The concept of individualism as a social idea — as distinct from legal, religious, or philosophical formulations — was virtually invented in the United States. Other countries, of course, had their share of individual egoism and selfishness. But it was in the United States where the ideology first triumphed that individuals and their needs were the principal objects to be served by the social order. As social scientists Seymour Lipsett and Everett Ladd put it, "Societies should be judged on the basis of how well they do in making people happy." In the social ideology of "Americanism," all the major elements — freedom, achievement, and even private property — support the central idea of individualism. People are to be free to be themselves, to act and develop in ways they find rewarding. They are to be judged on their individual achievements, not where they came from. Private property is to be protected not primarily because it motivates production but because it allows people the freedom to be themselves.

It is easy to see how such an ideology, however valuable, produces a people that increasingly sets its face against the social, the collective, and therefore the intimate. As America has developed, so has the notion of individual rights, so that more and more norms of social behavior — sexual taboos, for example, or taboos against the alteration of consciousness — have been thrown away. Consequently, an ever-increasing crowd of individuals follows Emerson's advice in *Self-Reliance*: "But do your thing." They do it, with fewer and fewer ties between them.

Even the physical conditions of American life have supported this tendency away from the intimate and toward the solitary. Ours was a continent to be explored and conquered. So we are a people for whom the road, some misty frontier, is always beckoning. Our impulse is to leave behind what is disagreeable and to move on in search of what is better. Older societies lack this sense of easy expansiveness and flight. Their limited space, town walls, ancient hedges, old fences, all cause restriction and conduce to more social notions of the individual's place. But we Americans scrap relationships that are not working as we would like — whether they be with relatives, with spouses, or with friends. We dispose of them like Kleenex. When it is inconvenient, painful, difficult, I get rid of you. I hit the road.

The road is not without its problems. Though it beckons with thrilling prospects of release from the past and bright new unknowns, it also fills us with fear. Not so much, anymore, the fear that we will meet hostile Indians or outlaws, but fear that nothing will be gained by following the road. Tomorrow, despite the change, will be like today. Hence one encounters in the numberless roadside diners and restaurants of America a curiously unstable mixture of emotions. The road holds a sense of excitement and adventure, a heroic looking forward into the dawn. And at the same time, as people eat their hamburgers and drink their coffee, they experience a strange depression and anxiety. Outside the windows, where six lanes of vehicles thrum the highway through night and day, the road leads nowhere. Necessarily, the exhilaration of sheer change collapses into the dread of continued emptiness.

As our era progresses, however, the spreading doctrine of individualism combines with the fascination of speed. The whole world begins to live the American experience of an endless frontier. Modern transportation allows, even compels, the patterns of easy separation that the American frontier once promoted. The personal automobile, perhaps more than any other technical invention, has broken the limited physical space in which human relating took place. Where before a people had to develop those habits of mind and heart that made relationships possible simply because they *were* enclosed, now those habits become irrelevant to the thrill of getting in a car and heading out.

Probably we only head out of town, after work, to suburban homes. But even there, nothing is static. Because immediately you must drive to a relatively distant shopping center. And then out of your suburb toward the airport and business engagements in strange cities or vacations in foreign countries. If your income and social status do not allow you quite so much locomotion, you wish they did. You envy the people who move the farthest and the fastest and you try to do so yourself, hoping each year to buy a more powerful car, or a second or third car, or a set of recreational vehicles.

All this movement consumes the personal energy and time that could be used for stable relationships. In addition, the possibility of covering great distances in relatively small amounts of time tends to destroy the spaces in which people might meet. Thus a modern house resembles a hotel or a waiting room more than a place of residence. People's lives are oriented not toward staying but toward anticipating the next trip or recovering from the last one. Families meet in an atmosphere of transport. Conversation around the table centers on plans for future travel. As each man's average daily radius expands, he has more and more trouble finding others. Part of the solution to our deep loneliness may have to do with giving up the opportunity for movement.

Still other technological achievements encourage the dissolution of human-sized spaces and relationships between people. The telephone is often a potent instrument for cutting us off from one another. Because it permits the illusion of instant communication, it helps us dwell at increasingly great distances from those we might love. But, as we all know, the telephone does not allow full communication between people; it allows only the exchange of information. Telephone conversations seldom carry real emotional power, a sense of truly being with the other person. But we use the telephone more and more to pursue what passes for our personal lives, and with less and less gratification.

The dehumanized quality of technology increasingly creeps into our very nature. The rise of reason as the dominant human function distances us from experience. At the start of modern culture, men began to admire machines and to try to imitate them. Large industrial organizations increasingly tended to treat workers like machines. High degrees of reliability, a tolerance for repetitiveness, a focus on work to the exclusion of nature or human feelings — all were held up as goals. Employees were not supposed to get tired, to lose their place in the organization chart, to get bored, to want variety.

With more clever management and a relaxation of the harsher types of exploitation, human vagaries are presently allowed, but only allowed. We now imitate the computer. Our deepest image of ourselves becomes man as rational producer, man identified with his mental processes, his brainpower.

Society teaches us to separate from our emotional, physical, and social nature and to behave according to the rules of a profession. Under such regulations, one performs increasingly limited rational operations, whether it is a matter of cutting up a body or a poem, a market profile or a mass of computations. Successful people in this system are able to perform reliably over a long period of time. Very successful people also manage, somehow, to preserve the outer shows of charisma, charm, magnetism, or whatever other qualities are conducive to being trusted and assigned leadership roles. In every case, however, the result is the same: one identifies with a socially cultivated mask the essential character of which is its lack of human depth and, most especially, its lack of depth of feeling. Can people under such discipline be true friends?

• • •

In the face of such social forces as rationalism, professionalism, economic and physical mobility, and individualism — all tending to destroy intimacy — modern people have attempted to substitute for the old tight fabric of relationships one relationship alone. Over the last two centuries, romantic love has come to be seen as something to which everybody, not just the rich person, is entitled. Moreover, romantic love, as the social historian Carl Degler has traced its evolution, has come to be seen as something one combines with marriage.

Most people's imaginations have come to be dominated by the idea of a lifelong, exciting intimacy with one person of the opposite sex. That this expectation is not universally realized does not stop people from trying. Despite the high divorce rate, a far greater percentage of the American population marries now than ever before.

In a world that tends to denature the emotional being, the modern man or woman clings to a spouse. It is not surprising, then, that most Americans will tell you their spouses are their best friends, although many more men will so declare than women. As a result, fear and guilt are attached to relationships outside marriage. When a man, for example, wants to go out at night with the boys, he doesn't just go; he tells them that first he must ask his wife whether their social schedule will allow it. There is no implied free social time for him other than that negotiated and granted by his wife.

A similar compact binds the woman, of course, although the women's movement has given women more liberty for outside relationships with their own sex than men now have. In essence, the man has become totally emotionally dependent on his wife. And because of changes in women's legal status and their increasing opportunities for professional work, a husband fears making a mistake. A wife can now afford to walk out on him, after all, and even take the children.

Increasingly, vital masculine energy that might be used to bond with another man is drained away. He may want the particularly adventurous flavor of male companionship, even deep friendship, but he is cautious about asking for it. The problem then arises that, as rich as his relationship with his wife may be, he eventually suffers from claustrophobia, from a sense of being suffocated in the arms of the Great Mother, an archetype he gradually projects on his spouse as his relationships with men become less vital.

Many women are aware of this pattern and occasionally encourage their husbands to seek male friends. But the social forces we have discussed stand in his way. The result, ironically, is that the wife finds her husband less interesting and adventurous than she wants and the husband experiences himself as a male failure, not sufficiently strong or adept enough even to implement his wife's simple, good advice. We are back, then, to the Great Mother and the kind of resentments that turn marital relationships sour.

All this tends directly to undermine the sexual life of the couple. Sexual attraction and excitation depend in part on perceived differences between partners, which are then bridged by the spark of sexual expression. When the sense of male and female difference becomes too diluted, as in many rather close and boring marriages, people get less sexy. The sexologist C. A. Tripp notes that "many women intuitively understand this refueling operation, and although they may miss their men who 'are off with the boys,' they use the time themselves to recuperate, correctly sensing that they are ultimate benefactors of men's diversion from them. Their hunch is right, as is the hunch of other women who feel a pensive disquietude with men who have no close male ties." In sum, if men had deep relationships with other men, their married sex lives would be better.

• • •

Part of the reason contemporary men attempt to put all their emotional and personal needs into the nest of romantic marriage comes from their deep feelings of hurt, shame, and guilt attendant upon the transitoriness and the failure of their earlier close male friendships. Because of all the historical forces we have noted, impermanence is typical of male friendships, as of all other relationships in our time. Some recent scholars of friendship, like the American psychologists John Reisman and Joel Block, urge us to accept such changes as a simple fact of modern life. They profess to be puzzled that the ancient ideal of "lifelong loyalty" in friendship be so much admired by people when, in fact, most friendships do not last a lifetime. They urge that people become more realistic, acknowledge that different friends serve different needs at different periods of life, and that this procession of more or less temporary relationships is a normal part of personal growth.

Valuing personal growth more than consistency in human relations is, of course, a strikingly modern stance. As an idea, it arises from the whole trend toward individualism and self-expression that marks the modern person, particularly the American. Unfortunately, the ideology of growth further helps to corrode human relationships: by putting individual growth over mutual association it helps to destroy the very idea of serious male friendship.

Somerset Maugham's *Of Human Bondage* gave a disturbing illustration of this tendency. The novel traces Philip Carey's adolescence and youth as he passes through various stages and beliefs — theism, aestheticism, pessimism — to find, eventually, some settled sense of self, symbolized by steady work in a modern profession and a loving marriage. At several points, however, Philip has to recognize that at every stage in his personal progress, he has left his friends.

At one moment, he is sitting in the British Museum, gazing upon the Greek tombstones of fifth-century Athens:

> There was one stone which was very beautiful, a bas-relief of two young men . . . It was an exquisite memorial to that than

which the world offers but one thing more precious, to a friendship; and as Philip looked at it, he felt the tears come to his eyes. He thought of Hayward and his eager admiration for him when they first met, and how disillusion had come and then indifference, till nothing held them together but habit and old memories. It was one of the queer things of life that you saw a person every day for months and were so intimate with him that you could not imagine existence without him; then separation came and everything went on in the same way, and the companion who had seemed essential proved unnecessary. Your life proceeded and you did not even miss him.

Similarly, Philip muses on a friend he had known in his artistic days, before he decided to become a doctor:

One evening about half past eleven he saw Lawson walking along Piccadilly; he was in evening clothes and might be supposed to be coming back from a theatre. Philip gave way to a sudden impulse and quickly turned down a side street. He had not seen him for two years and felt that he could not now take up again the interrupted friendship. He and Lawson had nothing more to say to one another. Philip was no longer interested in art . . . He was occupied with the forming of a pattern out of the manifold chaos of life, and the materials with which he worked seemed to make preoccupation with pigments and words very trivial. Lawson had served his turn. Philip's friendship with him had been a motive in the design he was elaborating: it was merely sentimental to ignore the fact that the painter was of no further interest to him.

It is not surprising that the novel ends with Philip in the arms of his bride but with no male friends in his life.

What Maugham doesn't say but so beautifully hints at is the tremendous sense of loss, of deep shame and dreadful mourning that is occasioned by these facile changes and sacrifices of earlier relationships. Relationships that exist in the male psyche under the sponsoring ideal of sacred loyalty to friends. Shame and mourning that are so bitter that one represses them. It is all very fine for the adult Philip to tell himself that avoiding Lawson is right and that anything else would be sentimental. But what has happened to the sentiments of affection, admiration, aspiration, of disappointment, shame, and guilt?

Our modern mobility, which separates men from one another in the most cruel ways, combines with our individualistic ideology of personal growth to litter our past with dead friendships. We rush to fill a puzzling emptiness with the love of women and with notions of our growth into rational adults.

All men know that these tactics don't entirely work. This changing and tearing up, particularly of masculine relationships, that were supposed to have an enduring strength about them, are corrosive to men's souls. So we come to doubt others and to hate ourselves. We come to doubt life itself. We can try to be "mature" like Philip. Or we can try to be the way many psychologists say we should be, telling ourselves that life is simply that way and that friends serve different functions at different times. So many tools for our living. But that is not at all, not at all what we had in mind for our male friendships.

But as the burden of guilt, shame, and disappointment accumulates over our youth, we, like Philip, bury our sadness and dissimulate our cynicism. After all, we can't spend the rest of our lives by ourselves. We continue to have friendly relationships with many people. Indeed, as we grow older, we get apparently less and less defensive, apparently more and more tolerant and easygoing. We reach out to new people with quick and ready smiles and hellos.

But though our strategies of repression and simulation work, allowing us to keep people in our lives, we are still lonely. Many American men will tell you they have friends. Some men will tell you that they are concerned about friendships. But nearly all men will confess that they want deeper, more profound friendships than they have. The burden of hurt from previous failures doesn't easily yield. It is this inner corrosion of the sentiments that makes so many men I have talked with explain the difficulty of making friends after youth with such phrases as "the organism hardens," "you get stiffer," "you become less open and less plastic." The masculine armor dissolved by earlier male friendships returns, lighter but tougher than ever. More precisely, the heart hardens from being pounded, stiffens from being hurt, and our distrust makes us sick with ourselves no less than with others.

Against this sickness some men may be driven to take action. They may slowly find themselves having to try to invent friendships that will suit the needs of their modern adult lives. My own quest was one of these.

3

First Essays in
Male Friendship

What is it like not to have a close friend?

Most men don't even notice. Docile, we have learned to accept our separation. But circumstances may arise that make us notice.

A wife, touched by the women's movement perhaps, begins to form serious engagements with other women. You hear her talking on the phone as you watch television at night. Politely, she gets up and closes the door so you won't be disturbed. But you are, somehow, even more disturbed. Occasionally you hear the sound of a peculiarly hearty laughter that you don't have in your own life, laughter of a kind that your wife doesn't even share with you. A shadow falls across your consciousness but you don't know exactly what to do about it. You respect her new friendships but you are envious.

Or you may get divorced. Now, suddenly, all the social time of life is strangely empty. Saturday night, Sunday morning. After five o'clock. You rush to fill this time with women, but they are not always available. Besides, you don't want to get serious now, not after all the recent pain. So you call up the couples you and your wife knew, but now that you are uncoupled there is awkwardness;

everybody behaves as if something, someone, is missing. The couples aren't sure how to treat your new women friends. Again, you find yourself alone.

Or your marriage is all right but sometimes you just want to go *out*. It is an almost animal urge, a muffled call of the wild in our civilized age. You want to drink, to have an adventure, to drive too fast, to discuss the visible virtues of women who pass. Something atavistic, you think to yourself, but still real. You call a man you know, but he only says, "Gee, that sounds great, but I've got some work to do tonight — big deal cooking at the office — let's do it another time." Except the other time doesn't come; he never calls back to suggest it; you think of calling yourself but somehow you want *him* to do it.

Or the experience is at a deeper level. You have your little group. Every week, you have a doubles game, or you play poker, or you go for a couple of drinks with the same guys. Then, suddenly, you have a real problem — a sick child, your job is in danger, your feelings about your wife are such that you can't stand yourself. But despite your regular male company, there is no one to talk to. So you consider getting yourself a psychiatrist, or joining an encounter group, or talking with a sympathetic woman at work. But you don't feel crazy, and you don't like groups, and you fear where that talk with the sympathetic woman might lead; right now, that's not at all what you need.

Or it may be more subtle. A very quiet and slow exasperation that builds up at work because you come to feel tired of not trusting anyone. On the way home you wonder who to talk with who will really understand, and you can't think of a soul. So you become aware of the ache of aloneness. Or a postcard from a foreign country is in the mail. Gratifying, but then you realize you haven't seen the vacationer in years. He's no part of your life now. Or you're working alone in your office on the weekend and you can't think another thought, but you don't feel like going home to the family. And yet, as you walk to your car, you notice that no one comes to mind to go and do something else with. So you get in the car and drive around, looking at women, looking at people, but your windows are rolled up tight.

A thousand little experiences, a multitude of minor longings, one or two major crises, may, in the case of some men, crystallize the discovery of an emptiness. In a certain few, it may lead to a longing for friendship, even to the idea of looking for a friend. Yet, men are taught not to talk about such things, not even to think about them. And, of course, that makes any search more difficult. For today there is a taboo on anything to do with friendship that smacks of deliberation.

Willie Morris has an elegantly phrased contempt for anything that smacks of the "art of friendship."

> You can train someone to kick a football or to take out an appendix but some things cannot be learned. If there is an esthetic to friendship, it exists in the reality and not in the effort. As with most of the complex achievements of life — sexual love, or tranquility, or the sensibility to comprehend that which is beautiful and passionate and true — friendship may even be God-given, and in this sense it is also a creature of accident and hence a rare blessing.

Of course, face it: either you're blessed or not, damned or not. There is nothing you can do about it. Such is the conventional wisdom. And I, like most men, instinctively agreed with it. Sure, friendship or love was always a "miracle," and the recent "art of friendship" books that Morris criticizes indeed strike one as vulgar and oversimple.

But enough had happened in my life that I had to make a try. It was an accumulation of problems and awareness: a divorce; resigning the presidency of a research institute and starting my own consulting business by myself; and something deeper, a sense that a closeness with one or a few other men, like the friendships I had had in college, but more adult, had finally to be put back in my life.

I found myself too deeply alone; starved, in a way. The time had come to find true friendship with other grown-up men.

I was dimly aware that I was seeking something special. I didn't yet have the words for it. But I knew I wanted something more than the carefully shallow relationships — at work, with couples, with tennis partners — that usually pass for friendship in the life of men. I wanted someone whom I liked very much and who felt the same way about me; I needed someone truly interesting; and I needed someone really open and trustworthy. My personal stakes were high.

A little timid, I began with men I already knew: halves of couples, a former coworker, a neighbor. I will return to these men I had known for fifteen years. For now I can only observe that the fact that *I* was tacitly prepared for a deeper relationship — more frequent, frank, and meaningful — did not automatically sweep us into something different from the limited understandings we had. I did not yet have any insight into the massive social forces that work against close relationships. Thus was I only aware that there seemed to be a mysterious, ineffable resistance to surpassing our normally limited interchanges. Our friendships seemed locked into old grooves, established at well-known levels. While we could get together and talk about old times or people we knew or even, occasionally, problems we were having, the relationships lacked depth. Naturally, I was afraid to talk about that.

At a certain moment, I decided to become more self-conscious about the whole matter. And when I decided to write a book about male friendship, I realized that giving myself the assignment would also give me courage and that the concentrated effort would help me find a worthy art of friendship. After all, I reasoned, it was not honorable to sit passively and wait at home for a miracle from God. When I felt the need of a woman's love, I sought it. So why not deliberately seek friendship with men?

Accordingly, against my own reticence and shyness, I began to push myself to look for possible new friends among the scores of people my work and my social network provided. I began keeping a journal lest I miss anything useful.

But most of the men I met didn't interest me. There was no resonance. It was only months after I began that I seemed to have what looked like a first success.

What follows are excerpts from my journal. This is what it was like for one man to try to find new, close friends at midlife.

[Harry Solano is a man somewhere in his early thirties whom I had met a few months before when I was looking for a job as a consultant with a community agency for which he occasionally volunteered as a business adviser.]

About One Year After My Divorce

Before today, I always used to describe Harry Solano by saying that he had the best manners of anyone I had ever met. His ways are as gentle as the soft brown leather of his hand-made shoes, the discreet roll of his custom-made lapels, the quiet of his dark eyes.

I had liked him and he had liked me, too. Or he seemed to. So, we've had lunch several times. Today, the San Francisco sun was especially perfect in the morning. One of those golden spring days you can have any time of the year: it wasn't really hot but by eleven o'clock you wanted to take your jacket off.

I had persuaded him to come out of the stony world of downtown, where he works as an executive in the family business. We met in one of those restaurants that is all bare wood and Boston ferns, a little chrome, a little glass, and peachlike waitresses. Ordinarily I don't like such places, but today's sun had seemed to wash the air, even inside, where it had not directly penetrated, so the phony naturalness of the place became, somehow, excused. It was not at all hard to be of good humor.

"How's the consultant business going?" Harry asked.

"I've got an assignment at Berkeley now." We talked about the job, he gave me advice, and I thanked him.

"Are you going to keep on with your family job or have you decided to go back to playing jazz?" I listened as he outlined his conflicts between the family tradition and his own interests, between the stability of staying where he had an assured place and striking out on his own. I gave him advice. He thanked me.

"What will you do after the consultancy?" he asked.

I told him my plans and worries, he gave me advice, I thanked him.

"What about your problems with your wife, your girl friend? Are you going to get divorced?"

We talked about his domestic situation. I gave him advice. He thanked me.

A normal, friendly California lunch. Pleasant enough. Open. Useful. But the words were not bearing well what was starting to exist between us. On the one hand there was my liking for this man. His sensitivity moved me: the kind smile, the soft dark eyes, a certain quiet attentiveness to everything I said or, I imagined, that anyone said. A natural delicacy had been bred up to a kind of human perfection. I want a friend like him. That is my reaction, on the one hand. On the other hand, I felt the banal California habit of easy self-disclosure, quick communication, facile questions about private matters, routinely understanding advice. The two hands did not quite meet and grasp one another.

The words, the questions and answers — what the local psychologists call sharing — were not quite satisfying. It didn't do justice to the tentative but real affection that I felt for Harry. Of course, I could tell him outright how I felt, but he already knew that without my saying so, and besides, I was certain it would not help at this point. All we seemed to be able to do was to be each other's helpers. Even each other's therapists. One might call it the importation of the professional attitude into the domain of private relationships. It's something you learn fast in these times. But this day, something in the air perhaps, something, was so perfect that mere friendliness, helpfulness, questions and answers gradually seemed unnecessary.

Our sentences became shorter. Soon the questions came less frequently. Each time the answers, despite the importance of the matters being discussed — jobs and love and future prospects — seemed less important.

I wouldn't have dared it myself. I wouldn't have quite known how to do it, so good a talker was I. But he, he had hung around musicians a lot and smoked a lot of dope. So once, when an answer hung in the air, inviting another question, he simply let it hang there. Silently, I followed him. After just a short time, we were two people, our bodies drawn up and touching the opposing wooden edges of our table, chins in hands and elbows propped, just sitting together.

Quiet.

When lovers sit, they stare into eyes and see whole worlds revealed. They burn and they ache with the desire for what the other is. They are drawn, pulled, even when they don't move — like the lovers in Donne's "Ecstasie."

This was different. What was happening had no particular pull or tension. Our eyes would brush past each other. Manly, we suppressed our possible embarrassment and the desire to laugh, or to twitch, or simply, Jesus Christ, to say something to interrupt the silence. No, we both kept quiet. The old-fashioned wooden fan turned around in the light fixture above us. The waitresses made their ways past other tables. Knives and forks scraped elsewhere. But we were silent.

There was an excitement. Diffused. I could feel it all over my body. I kept looking, as people predict these days, for something sexual, but no, not that. It wasn't in my genitals. It wasn't anywhere, exactly. But exciting.

I would have giggled, I guess, at the double pleasantness, of experience and discovery, but I had enough good sense to control myself, to keep returning to the discipline of quiet. Of being together. Of sharing this silence that, somehow, we had created together. A sort of mutual achievement, that took its continued existence from the willed act of letting be.

Then, someone spoke. I can't remember who — me or Harry or the waitress.

We had known that it wouldn't last forever. That had been one of the pleasures. The sense that time was racing eternity before the rhythm of one's quiet breath.

We paid the check. We got up. We walked to Harry's car. We smiled and shook hands. We knew the tender value of what had happened. But we didn't speak about it. In my mind, I thanked him for knowing how to shut up. It was only a brief experience.

The Next Day

I am pleased with myself. Yesterday wouldn't have happened had I not forced myself to call Harry. Before I would not have called. I had pretty well given up on making new friends. So we wouldn't have met for lunch. I would have waited for a miracle. Instead, I pushed a little and I got the miracle.

The silence we shared made me remember something I had known but forgotten. Intimacy is one of the basic beauties of life.

Of course. Everybody knows that. But I had forgotten. When people get on top of life, successful and rich, what do they turn themselves toward? Beauty. Philosophy and the spiritual life. And intimacy: people. They turn toward people. Striving in my thirties for a little success, I had forgotten in a real way what intimacy was about — its textures and delights.

I know Harry had the same experience today. I think our friendship has begun.

About Six Weeks Later

"Hello, Mr. Solano's office!" Harry's secretary is always a little officious, even surly. Wrongheadedly, I take it personally that Harry's secretary is surly when I call. But I can't call him at home because he's just moved out and I don't know where he's moved to. I would complain about Juanita's surliness but I know that nothing can be done.

"This is Stuart Miller, Juanita. Is Harry there?"

"Mr. Solano is out of the office right now, Mr. Miller," she snaps.

"Could he call me when he gets in?"

"I'll certainly give him that message, Mr. Miller!"

"Thank you."

"Don't mention it, Mr. Miller."

Three Days Later

"Hello."

"Hello, Stuart, it's Harry. Listen, I'm sorry. I've been so swamped I couldn't call you back sooner."

"I understand, Harry. I know you're having a lot of trouble. I just wanted you to know that I am ready to help in any way I can." I don't know what else to say, because I don't really know the guy. I've never been to his house. I've never met his wife. We were going to do all that but then things exploded for him. "Let's get together."

I can hear Harry flipping the pages of his calendar.

"That sounds great, Stuart. But not this week. I've got to spend the weekend with my kid. Then we've got the family meeting — with my parents. And then there's my wife."

"Are you still seeing your girl friend?"

"Yes, it's going well."

"I'm glad." I was glad something was going well for him.
"Listen. How about next Friday? Not this one, the one after?"

"O.K." I say, a little disappointed.

He catches it. "It's too bad it's so long before we can get together. But you will understand, I hope."

"Of course, Harry, of course."

Nine Days Later

"Hello."

"Hello, Mr. Miller? This is Juanita Briggs, Mr. Solano's secretary. Mr. Solano says to say he is very sorry but he can't make lunch on Friday. He has to go out of town. He hopes you will understand. He'll call you when he gets back."

"Can I speak to him?"

"I'm afraid he's in a meeting right now."

"Well, give him my best."

"I certainly will, Mr. Miller!"

Three Weeks Later

"Gee, I'm sorry I'm late, Stuart. I hope you haven't been waiting too long." He looks, distracted from his hurry, around the restaurant.

"About twenty-five minutes. I don't mind." And I don't quite; it's just that I can't seem to get together with this guy.

We speak mostly about Harry.

About his wife.

About his kid, who is sick.

About his girl friend.

About his job plans.

About his psychiatrist.

"What are you going to do?" I ask.

"I don't know, but I have a feeling everything will work out."

"I have the same feeling, Harry. Everything will work out."

A Month Later

"Hello, Stuart? I'm sorry it took me so long to get back to you.
Yes. Everything is all right. But I've got to go on a trip. I'm
sorry I didn't call. You know how it's been."
  "I know."
  "Let's get together when I get back."
  "Sure. Want to make a date?"
  "I can't just now. I'll call you."

Our relationship never stopped being that way. First that
wonderful silent opening to one another in the restaurant. Then.
Then, what? Even now, I don't really know. The easiest explanation, I suppose, is that Harry just didn't have time for a new friend.
  But I don't think it was a question of time. After all, Harry
may work, but he has millions of dollars of his own. He can make
time better than almost anyone. He can cut down on his job. He
has all the time in the world. And while other people aren't as rich,
many can also rearrange priorities, delegate, cut back, hire and
shuffle. If they want to. Rather, I discovered that friends and
friendships just weren't as important as the other items on Harry's
agenda.
  Nothing personal, probably. He made it clear that he liked me.
  I know that I kept trying, at least doing the basic work of
making the phone calls and booking the lunches, being persistent.
But we never got anywhere close to the intimacy of that special
afternoon. Harry was running distracted. The few times we met,
we exchanged information aplenty, but the real being together
didn't happen again. In a way, it was a miracle it had happened at
all. Who expects the formal lunch, sandwiched between business
appointments, to yield any deep pleasure? And without pleasure,
what basis is there for friendship?
  My feelings became hurt: I even became offended that I was

doing almost all the work of keeping our relationship alive. A year after that special lunch, frustrated with both the infrequency of our meetings and their lack of depth, I wrote Harry a letter, asking him what had happened. Its tone was a little angry but I mentioned I was very open to renewing things. This was more of the art of friendship, trying to clarify the situation hoping that we could go forward again. I never received a reply. Apparently, with quiet homicide, he gradually did away with our nascent friendship. And I will never know why. If, indeed, there is a why.

About Four Months After the Famous Lunch with Harry Solano

It is the moment to review my relationship with Ronald Sutherland Richard Byrd. A mutual acquaintance introduced us some months ago. Mostly at my instigation, we have had several dinners at a neighborhood Chinese restaurant. Interested in and for years high in the professional side of the art world, he is slim, soft-spoken, and charming. He wears pale jeans, Italian turtlenecks, and smokes thin cigarillos from Holland. He interlards his conversations with French expressions. Pretentious? Phony? Maybe.

But I rather like his elegance: the quiet drawl, the air of calm and infinite time. And I like the fact that, like me, he has done many jobs and been a part of many worlds.

I also like Ronald's eccentricity. The kitchen of his modest rented house is a McLuhanesque exhibition. Newspaper clippings bearing the visual and print symbols of the age cover the walls in some arcanely revelatory order.

Our telephones often separate rather than join us. When I feel a warm, friendly impulse to call Ronald, it is worse than calling Harry Solano. Ronald has incorporated and operates a nonprofit affair out of his house, and his phone is monitored by a cheap answering machine that plays the same recording, now baritone, now soprano: "No one is here to answer your call right now," begins the elegant voice. "If you will kindly leave your name, number, and the purpose of your call" — the recording begins to mount in speed and pitch — "one of us will call you back" — and finishes in a kind of muffled scream.

Last night Ronald and I had another Chinese meal together.

"I think I've found you a job."

"Marvelous, *mon vieux*." Ronald carefully pours himself a glass of the house white from a frosty carafe.

"A cultural organization I know is looking for an executive. I think it suits you."

"Perfectly. My very best thanks to you." He raises his glass in acknowledgment. "How shall we explore the matter?"

We discuss the details just as we had previously discussed other matters of business: consulting jobs for one of us, possible book projects, courses to teach, possible trips to Europe. Both of us moving into our forties, we were used to exchanging tips, tactics, and strategy in friendly fashion, all the while looking for the next directions of our lives.

Last night, however, I was after something simpler between us. It is time to get beyond our parade of past and future achievements, time for something more personal.

I waited until the business had exhausted itself. The check had already come. But there was still time. How to nudge us forward, to get behind the mask of our mutual competence?

"What's going on with you, Ronald?" I ask as tentatively as I can. "Apart from the various projects, what moves you? What troubles you? What are you afraid of? I know that you are not the type to talk easily about such matters, but I want you to know that I am interested. I like you."

Ronald's head edges backward, very slightly, as I speak. He pours himself another glass of wine. Again, with great care. Meditating his reply.

"And I like you, too, Stuart." He stares quietly at me, as if to say that this was all I will get. That it is too soon for him, would perhaps always be too soon, with his southern ways.

But he also doesn't want to turn me away too roughly. I can see that. He looks at me with his cool gray eyes. "Why, what is going on with me is the same as has been going on for twenty years: meditation, music, history — I am in ecstasy nearly all the time!"

Ronald smiles at me.

I take the signal to rise, questioning my judgment in picking this particular man to try and be friends with. I like him. I even respect his aloofness and reserve. But I wonder if it will be possible to go further. Still, I need a friend and he's got a lot of good qualities. I will try again. All this trying to make friends is new to me; I am not really sure how to do it.

The Next Morning

Yesterday's journal is false. I am leaving out too much. I am writing, some days, as if all this deliberate trying to make a new friend is something easy for me.

But, in fact, when I sat in the restaurant and asked Ronald about his real feelings, I had to force myself to do it. I sit watching the cool, charming Southerner and I want to know what is really going on with him. But then, I think, as he looks at me with his quiet smile, there's nothing. He is a happy, self-contained character, a man who knows himself and is at peace. But what am I? A strange kind of needy creature, with hankerings after some sort of closeness that others don't seem to require. Wanting to be known, to share something, a brother, trust — I'm not even sure I know what it is that I want, much less how to get it. And what will the other man think? He will, he does, slight me after I put myself forward. My pride is put into question by this needing and reaching. I know these feelings and I must fight them all the while that I do this crazy thing. It is heroic, in a small way, what I am doing. I know that, too.

It was a measure of the sunken estate of men's friendship that I finally got a hint from a young professional, a graduate of the women's movement, about how to advance my friendship with Ronald. She's got close women friends.

About Two Weeks Later

"You've got to up the ante," she tells me.

I look blank.

"In a way you did it when you asked Ronald about his feelings. But he didn't bite. Put yourself forward again: more chips on the table. Raise the stakes! I've done it — had to do it — with my new friends these last years. Comes a point where a new relationship sticks. You've met, you like the person, you get together for lunch. But nothing more happens. So, somebody has to move in on the other in some way.

"Of course," she finished dryly, "you can get hurt."

Ten Days Later

Ronald and I are sitting in our usual Chinese restaurant and I am thinking about what he mentioned ten minutes earlier: "My landlord is reclaiming his house. I shall have to move my furniture, the ten thousand books in the library, everything, to another location."

"What a disaster."

"It will be, *mon vieux*, as they say, 'a pain in the ass.' "

"Will you have movers?" I am a little worried, because I know that at the moment Ronald has little money.

"My landlord's teenage sons will lend a hand, *mon ami*," he replies with apparent good cheer.

It is clear that despite the enormous disruption and labor, Ronald is not going to become visibly upset. The thought has already occurred to me that if I were trying to be his friend, I should help him move. But I hesitate to offer. Not only because it will be hard work and take time. But largely because he hasn't asked me to help.

Here is the concern about independence again.

In college, when we were all poor, and in the years right afterward — the years when we had friends — it was expected that friends helped one move. It was nearly ritualistic: schlepping the same shabby furniture from one shabby apartment to another shabby apartment. And then the ritual wall painting: always off-white.

But we are grown-up now. We have valuable furniture — even antiques, a large library, an oil painting or two. Such possessions tell our success in life. We are supposed, therefore, to be independent, to have enough money of our own to pay for others to move us. In that sense, we don't need anybody — anybody in particular, at least. The declaration of wants, the exchange of needs that lay the groundwork for human association — men in war, farmers raising a barn, people needing emotional support — this is not for real men anymore. It is beneath us.

At our age, the proper arena of male friendship is the comfortable meal, or the golf course, or perhaps certain kinds of work. But not that involvement with one another's very lives. Besides, I'd probably pull my middle-aged back. Ridiculous.

So I watch Ronald sip his brown tea and say nothing.

The Next Morning

The first thing I did was get up and call Ronald's answering machine. I told that irritating appliance that I wanted to help him move and that I would be available when he wanted. Half an hour later Ronald called back, pleased, and told me to come over tomorrow at noon. The ante is upped: I feel proud of doing this and a little silly.

The Night of the Following Day

It has been an extremely complex day.

I had forgotten, first of all, the boredom. When you do something physical and practical with someone, there is the quotient of boredom that goes with all work. The minutes ticking by as we stare at a wall of books and wonder how to begin to pack them and move them, for instance. It is a different boredom from what comes when friendship has as its exclusive theater the meal at home or in a restaurant. There, the boredom is subtler and runs deeper — frustration that conversation never leaves certain grooves, that we engage at the level of social persona even when we appear to be exchanging personal confidences. Such boredom is always dissimulated: hidden by the bright smile, the concerned look, chitchat. We know we are expected to be entertaining to our friends. But moving Ronald, boredom came naturally and frankly, because all physical activity involves down time, emptiness. So side by side, Ronald and I were bored. It was a forgotten kind of being together.

Despite this, the move was mainly an intense affair for me. I had not realized before how our houses are arranged like stage sets. Colors emphasize, dramatize, impress. Shadows conceal what we would hide, lighting illuminates what we would promote. Furniture is arranged to harmonize, to give an impression of order, of solidity, of taste.

And no more careful arrangement than in Ronald's housecenter which he had laid out as a kind of museum.

But I can tell you, I who had efficiently ripped the bedclothes from where he sleeps and folded them for transport, that beneath Ronald's comforter is a silken coverlet, and that coverlet hasn't been washed or cleaned in years. I know that because the stain of menstrual blood in the middle of it has the unmistakable hue of aged oxidation forgotten. I can tell you that in the corners of his closets are small clumps of old, dirty socks. That beneath the sofa no vacuum has penetrated to lift the gathering wool of dust.

The elegant Southerner is dirty. He cares more for the appearance of his walls and buying a new art book than to have his bedding cleaned. Suddenly, I know this much more about Ronald. It relieves some of the anxiety I feel about his apparent cool perfection. But it makes me wonder, again, if one with so much front is a man I should trust.

In general, however, such relevations strengthen my feelings for Ronald rather than warn me off. I accept with gratitude the intimacy that being a mover-friend allows me. I am learning.

In the middle of the afternoon, Ronald's ex-wife arrives to drop off their son for the weekend. The mother already turning to fat. A pretty, vague face. The parents speak in that peculiarly civilized way of ex-spouses in an enlightened age: a severely guarded kindness. She was not sufficiently brilliant for him, I think. That is the reason for their divorce. The child is leggy and restless at five years. Beautiful, energetic, gifted with Ronald's intelligence. The child may crack before age ten from the deep tensions underlying his parents' relationship, from the contrary currents of genes they have given him, or the child will be spectacular, brilliant, and whole. I see the father's best qualities in the child.

Then I meet the housemate. Earlier in the day Ronald has said, "I'll kill him."

"Why?"

"I've spent fifty hours, the last few days, arranging my few hundred best books in the living room of the new house. Last night, Tom came back and moved those three bookcases, pushed all the books back in a row. I am seldom angry, *mon vieux,* but you shall see it today!"

I see neither anger nor what damage the housemate has

caused. Apparently, Ronald has some secret arrangement he likes for these special books. They are placed as for an exhibit — the art man, again — but Tom had pushed them all back into an ordinary phalanx of books in cases. But there is no explosion when the luckless roommate appears. Ronald takes him aside and there is only earnest, quiet conversation. So I learn that Ronald can't get simply angry. Another discovery.

Most of it, however, measured by sheer clock time, was just the old remembered schlepping. Gathering in arms, bending and flexing, and coming back for more. All afternoon, a labor of love. A gift to a friend, a boring duty. The worry about slipping a disk. The pleasure of hard work together.

Later, Ronald and I and the child went for pizza. The sun was setting; the fog had come in. The work was finished and it was cool. We stuffed ourselves and he insisted on paying. I let him. Gift to gift. I had labored and he acknowledged the help. Pizza and beer and the bored, tired little child. It was more than our Asian meals together. It could be the beginning of being together. My efforts, for such they are, at friendship with him are leading somewhere. Though I have not really penetrated Ronald's aloofness. He seems far away still. Probably anxiety about the move. Which he will not admit. But it has been a good day.

Eight Months After Moving Ronald

As I take stock of what has resulted from all this trying over the past year, I find that the move is the last moment I remember about my relationship with Ronald. After that, I am not sure we even saw each other again. I know that there were exchanges of messages, on his answering machine and with my answering service. That we both began traveling and missing each other's calls. That I seemed to do most of the initiating of these flurries of calls — or is that merely my imagination, my oversensitivity to slight, my masculine measuring of who did what for whom and how much each invested and did I do more?

I remember feeling angry at not hearing from him for long stretches, but was it all his fault? Or did I realize, in some half-conscious way, that the bloodstain and the dirty socks, hidden except for the extraordinary occasion of moving houses, would be all the revelations I would get? That the exhibits would go up in the new dwelling. That each of the hundreds of volumes would be exquisitely arranged in the new living room, forever. And that there would be, fundamentally, only the elegant coolness, the southern-gentleman reserve, the permanent withdrawal. In short, that I would always sense that something was being withheld but never be allowed to know what it was.

Perhaps *I*, at last, unconsciously withdrew from *him*.

I am not sure. In any case, the experience was one of a vague, mysterious impasse. The person who introduced us told me the other day that he, too, had not heard from Ronald. "He's simply disappeared."

I found actual comfort in that. I had also feared that Ronald was just another man who had, perhaps, found me uninteresting. Perhaps that is also the case. Or maybe Ronald is too busy struggling to make a living to have the energy or courage for new friends. Being middle-aged these days seems to make it hard to keep entirely afloat. In all dimensions, one gets waterlogged and one's own heaviness can become all one can manage. In any event, I'm not going to call that answering machine to find out. I've put myself out enough. And I don't want my feelings hurt again.

Please don't get me wrong. I didn't get excited about every man I met and want to make friends with him. But I had taken it on as something I needed to do and would do. I met hundreds of people that year but tried to be friends with only four men. Harry and Ronald you have heard about. Ulysses Grant Richardson, a banking executive and former White House scholar, and Norman Goldberg, an unemployed research economist from New York, just come out to the Coast following his wife and her more successful career, were the other two.

I suppose that Richardson surprised me the most of all. An old acquaintance had suggested we meet socially. Richardson had helped arrange a loan for my old research institute years before, and one day, he invited me to his house for lunch.

The house was a stone hybrid between a samurai warrior's lodge and a Gothic cathedral. You could tell that a very expensive California architect, probably at the beginning of a career that would become more sober with time, had been permitted to let himself go. It was beautiful and imposing, but one wondered if one would really be up to living among its vaults and clearstories, its cruciform floor plan and its curving beams.

The man for whom it had been built was less fancy in appearance but equally monumental and impressive. Six feet six with legs like the proverbial trunks, his head massive and solid, his chest thick with the exercises of past youth. On the wall of his study was a photo-poster of his quite beautiful blond wife. Otherwise, everything was big: the antique French desk at which he worked, the views from the windows, the Chinese, French, and Italian dictionaries with which he pursued his current linguistic and philological hobby.

Richardson gave me a light lunch with a casually chosen heavy French wine. Then he told me he thought male friendship an insufficiently important topic for a book. He preferred subjects more in the great tradition, he said, something on the order of "the good life" or "justice." "There are too many books already on all kinds of secondary subjects," he said. Apart from this heavy thrust — which I put down to the bad habits of businesslike combativeness — he was cordial and charming. He talked of language and mythology and history and joked about the sloppy habits of English usage with which his California psychologist acquaintances tortured him. I learned he was active not only in his profession and hobby but also on the boards of half a dozen good-works organizations. I came away feeling very impressed, a little put down, and even quite outclassed.

With much surprise, then, did I receive the following letter about a week later:

Dear Stuart:

I propose that you and I avowedly continue what I think has already begun, a friendship of our own. I like you very much: I feel good in your company. In particular I feel my intelligence and my humor appreciated, a reception which is not so frequent and which I miss. So often I feel my sense of humor is in isolation: in consequence when the experience of shared amusement occurs, I'm delighted.

In any case, onward. What's next? Do women get into this? I'd certainly like you to know Harriet and the children. You've already met the dogs. What about lunch solo in a few days?

Dir Freundschaft willens,

Ulie

I was moved. Not merely because I had set him upon so high a pedestal (high as the roof beams of his house) and he had seen me as being on the same level. That, of course, was comforting, even flattering. But I was even more impressed by his courage to declare, particularly in writing, that he wanted a friendship. This was an exemplary piece of masculine forthrightness. I had come to know how it was natural for men, myself included, to be timid and evasive in this matter. Here was a man who could be a worthy friend. I called him at once.

Alas, in its general outlines, the rest of the story was already familiar. Several lunches, phone calls returned less and less often;

then, personal problems for Ulysses, including divorce from the beautiful wife and separation from house, children, and dogs. I called him repeatedly, told him I was available to help, invited him over. He could never find time to come. I think he turned for support in his crisis to a men's group with whom he had been meeting for two years. I'm not sure; he had always treated the group with irony when I asked him about it. Then, I remarried.

Maybe we started at the wrong time, he and I. Even putting all these life changes aside, the few times we did get together — in the usual luncheon restaurants — face to face, he just didn't seem able to deliver on the promise of his letter. He would give mini-lectures on what struck him as the more absurd points of English usage in California. He would snort: "What does 'It doesn't feel right to me' really mean?" Bored with his business, unable or perhaps afraid to feel with me, a relative stranger, the disasters that had overtaken him, he grasped for philology and hoped that because of my English professor background I would play. But such defensive games had long since ceased to interest me.

As with Harry and the minutes of silence, so with Ulysses. We never again reached the heights of the initial excitement. This happened even though both of us, presumably, worked at the art of friendship, treated the new relationship in a careful and deliberate fashion. Another puzzling disappointment.

With Norman Goldberg it had been different from the first. Norman was a *Landsman,* a short, red-haired and hyperactive New York Jew who spoke several modern languages, kept up in art, social science, theater, and three dozen other fields, laughed a good deal, and generally behaved like Mel Brooks with a Ph.D. His tall girl friend, whose book I was editing as a consultant job, had thought to introduce us because Norman was "new to San Francisco and would need friends." We met for the first time, as by now seemed inevitable, over lunch at a restaurant. We laughed together. I was also tacitly sympathetic about Norman's being in a new town and out of work. He insisted on ordering and we ate very well and generally had a rousing time.

But every meeting after that was a disaster. Norman revealed himself to be totally different from the jolly, outgoing intellectual I had first thought him to be. Norman the crude; Norman the insulting; Norman the self-involved and self-important, a "narcissist" — a word he used later — of the highest class. So smashing was the disillusionment, so gagging his offensiveness, that I tried hard, for several months, simply not to believe it. I put it down to his anxiety at not yet having a job; to his East Coast sharpie ways, which would fade with time; to my own lack of something. I wasn't sure what. Except it never stopped.

Finally, without telling him, I made my decision to fade from his life. I knew I should have confronted him — as Harry and others had not confronted me — with my reasons. But I told myself I just didn't have the stomach to endure more abuse. So, gradually, I returned his phone calls later and later. I dragged out the possibilities for future meetings, claiming wife and family matters, business. In short, with anger, malice, and some real shame at doing it this usual way, I just disappeared, as others had seemed to disappear on me.

• • •

What did I learn from that year of trying to make new friends? In a word, despite what the new "art of friendship" books say to the contrary, it is *not easy* to go out and make real friends after the age of thirty-five. Even when, as I did, you have the interest, the deep desire, and the will. Even when, as I did, you pick with care men of similar interests, similar senses of humor, similar intellectual and cultural backgrounds. Even when you plug away at it with all sincerity, when you make two or three phone calls for every one you receive, when you go to the extent of reviving juvenile behaviors like assisting, unasked, in a household move. Even when you begin with great mutual excitement, when the beginning is marked, as in the case of Harry Solano, by an incident that reorients your own notion of what is important in life. Even when Ulysses Richardson declares himself on paper — an astonishing act in this cautious age, where personal transitoriness is considered so normal that sentiments are rarely entrusted to paper. Even when, with the exception of Norman from New York, the men you choose are all basically California softies, with repressed senses of aggression and competition, with hundreds of hours of therapy and groups to help them relate successfully and openly to other new people. Even when you have tried, within your own prejudices, a range as varied as rich businessman-musician, art professional, philological banking executive, and unemployed economist.

Even when you have met all these conditions and tried all these approaches, it is hard to make friends after thirty-five. Above everything, there is no natural matrix out of which friendship can easily arise and establish itself.

We meet in restaurants, as if on neutral terrain, in between what we take to be the real business of life. Friendship is a luxury, an incidental. It no longer occupies the honored natural ground of community, piazza, shared manhood. So, better to have made friends professionally. Perhaps. But these four men, and most of the others I interviewed, did not have true friends at work. The kind of disinterested and deeply engaged friendship I was seeking seldom occurs there.

I came to feel that without a proper modern institution of friendship, with friendship accorded its own high standing and honor, the frail attachments that had flowered between myself and Solano, Sutherland, and Richardson were easily blighted. I would call, they would not be at the phone because of other concerns, and my call would become another item on the day's list, subject to time management. With children, home, errant wives, demanding lovers, and work — all automatically coming before friendship and me — it is no wonder that I wasn't quickly called back, and sometimes not at all. But with my new awareness of wanting deeper friendships, I found time to call them. I made it. I kept at it despite my own list of pressing obligations.

Of course, in a sane society and in all Western societies until the present, the claim of friendship would have been heard as loudly as many, if not all, of the aforementioned concerns of men. I know that sounds like heresy, but it was always so until now. In the Western tradition, loyalty to friendship and to male friends historically had as great a value as wife, work, and children. Male friendship was, like these others, an essential institution.

When I myself rejected the offensive Norman, the exclusion could be so simple because it took place without a social matrix and without the background expectations of a publicly esteemed institution. I simply disappeared into the wires of my answering service as others had disappeared. I vanished into my private calendar of things-to-be-done that could not include him, even though he called and insisted; I had my "conferences to attend," "clients to see," "business trips," "reports to write," "an engagement with my wife that night," and so forth. I dropped him and moved on, without any social need to offer a real explanation.

Such easy and convenient disappearing acts, whether we practice them upon others or they upon ourselves, are thoroughly modern and literally maddening. When someone drops out of a relationship, just like that, you have a tendency to think you are crazy.

You stand there clutching empty space where before there was somebody. A friend. That is, of course, a foolish position. Being a rational animal, you begin to think. You begin to wonder what it was that brought you to such a pass. You begin to imagine that you must be insufficiently smart to be liked or perhaps insufficiently something else. Or is it, as you think in what you believe to be your saner moments, that the fault is in the absence of a social matrix and an institutional context for friendship?

Tossed by such doubts, you can, if you allow it, easily give way to increasingly violent imaginings about your lack of worth. How many of us have done this in darker moments? If you do, you can vaguely sense others making similar gestures, quietly muttering the same doubts.

These are not pleasant experiences. Shame and guilt accompany them, more loneliness and disillusionment to strengthen the male armor. No one would take it amiss if you stopped trying and just clutched your own shoulders, calmly now, without a peep, without ever again reaching out to others in a serious way. In dejected moments, I felt like giving up.

Yet the thought persisted that Willie Morris, while certainly on to something, could not be wholly right. We cannot simply be doomed to await the miracle of friendship in a society that seldom offers it. My failures had at least taught me that if you are interested in reviving the possibilities of friendship, you have to avoid thinking it will be straightforward, easy, fast, or painless. Almost everywhere I looked, I found friendship dead, the very idea not taken seriously. To steer through such rough chaos would clearly require a wise and a patient art, perserveringly practiced and fed by irrational faith. To revive true friendship was also going to require tough persistence, struggle, and more knowledge than I yet had.

I turned for possible enlightenment to the few men I encountered who, oddly, seemed to have significant relationships.

4

Three Men

It has been remarked that we moderns lack literary models for deep friendship. That while there are many great love stories in modern literature, there is little about friendship at all. David and Jonathan, Pylades and Orestes, Roland and Oliver, Amis and Amilie — those loyal pairs of heroes — lack modern literary equivalents, a fact that tends to undermine the possibility of finding friendship in life.

We have no literary examples of friendship because friendship has lost its modern dignity. But there are some friendships out there in the great world. By the end of the second year, I had asked hundreds of men about their friendships. Despite most men clearly admitting that they had no real male friends and most of the rest pretending or thinking they did when they did not, I found a few friendships.

The three accounts that follow are no high literature of contemporary friendship. They are, instead, records of rather ordinary men trying to talk about their relationships with an engaged listener. Most of us, including these men, are not poets, and we cannot, in so many words, express exactly *what* is important to us. Nor are these three men heroic figures whom one is spontaneously moved to imitate. They are not models, and their friendships are not even of the highest we can conceive.

But they are real. And every reader will find his own particular meanings in them just as I found my own. More generally, for our forlorn times, they are harbingers of possibilities, evokers of the archetype, notes toward which one can tune oneself. They help alleviate the shortage of points of reference in contemporary literature. If we have the imagination to read the following accounts with open hearts and an eye to what is implied rather than always stated, we can use them. For, as I came to feel in my own frustrating quest, it is not so much that a new literature of friendship is needed. We need, most urgently, to build in the air of our own imagination, individually and together, the possibilities for a renewal of friendship. In this task, the contemplation of such friendships as do exist can help.

· · ·

Scott Deering was not unusual to look at. At home he dressed like a type of New Englander: moccasins, chino pants. His glasses were steel framed and his blond hair was straight and shiny atop his six feet. But he was unusual in that he *wanted* to talk about his friendships. Most men are reluctant to talk very much about the subject. Friendship is generally held to be something touchy, sacred, and manly, better kept behind tight lips. But Scott, having heard from his wife, an old acquaintance of mine, that I was working on the subject, quietly insisted on being interviewed. She had already told me that he was atypical in that he still maintained an involvement with a group of childhood comrades, even though he was nearing forty and they were all scattered across the country. Within that group, he had a couple of particularly important friendships, she said, though it was the life of the group that had first established the basis for those special adult relationships.

Scott first wanted me to know why this group had managed to survive when most other American men had lost their childhood comrades. He began analytically. Gradually, as I brought him to answer more specific questions about its palpable being rather than its underlying meaning, the group came to have for me something of the life it had for him.

"Above all, the friendships were not professional," Scott told me. "They had no purpose. No specific goal or activity such as characterizes work relationships. In my middle twenties, when I was working very, very hard to get started, I was close to a number of other lawyers. It was an arrangement based on shared interests of a particular kind. With my friends in the old group, however, any topic, any activity, is possible. This breadth is critical.

"Another reason it's survived is the traditions. We began and it flourished most when we were between twelve and eighteen. We built institutions."

I was excited at the idea and asked him exactly what he meant.

He stopped, surprised that I didn't know by intuition what was so clear to him. "Well. At one point we decided to have a reunion every ten years and we did. In 1968, everybody showed up; and in seventy-eight, again, including one guy we hadn't seen in ten years, and that was tragic. Or we used to elect the 'loser' of the summer, the person who had most screwed up, and we still do. Once, when we forgot, we even did it on the telephone, afterward. And the card game on Saturday night. And, most essential, getting together every summer, even now, though I live in one state and the other five are scattered all over the country."

He fell into silence, but I wanted him to tell me more of what was so vivid to him. So deep is the taboo against men's talking about what is important to them that even though he had volunteered to speak, I had continually to coax him into expression. I dissimulated the depth of my interest lest my concern rebound and provoke still further his natural New England reticence. All I did was press him with questions, intently but with a deliberate factuality.

"Where did all this take place? What is the actual setting?"

"It's a lakeside resort where everybody's parents went for the summer. During the winter, we were all away at private schools. So in the summer, the lake was our community."

"What's it like?"

"It's a lake. Well, it's eight miles long."

"If you look at it, what do you see?"

"Some small sailing boats, a yacht club. People live around the lake in different places, and we used to take motorboats to see one another. There was tennis and water-skiing, parties and sailing. We all first met, over twenty years ago, at the yacht club. When we were kids, we would take the chairs up, white wooden folding chairs, so we could get into the dances for free."

"Tell me more about the lake."

He looks baffled for a moment but agrees, his head and his thick shoulders nodding his final acquiesence.

"There's a road around it. Gravel. Hasn't changed much since I was a kid. An Interstate came by about ten years ago, but you would hardly know it's there. The trees hid it. Maybe the trees are bigger now. The houses are still small, three-bedroom summer homes. All have been enlarged since those years. But it's hard to see the houses because of the trees."

"Trees and hills and water," I summarize, leading him, "pines and maples and oaks?"

"Yes."

"And when you get together now?"

"Now, we don't go to the yacht club on Saturday night as we used to. We go to the house we used to visit on Sundays. Two brothers in the group own it now, and it has a big square table. It's interesting — back then, the kids brought the parents together. It was us. And the parents still see each other, they go back every summer, too."

"That's pretty unusual these days, a two-generational community that supports friendships."

Scott suddenly wants to plunge on. Now he wants me to see the essence, which, under my prodding, is slowly becoming evident to him. "It was a community, as you say, but it was different from any one I've known since. Different even from the college community, which offered its own support for friendships. You see, it was all in the summer. A hot, heavy, timeless season when, at that age, there was nothing to do, nowhere to go, nothing to prove. I suppose you could say that the lake symbolizes its very purposelessness. Clear, empty, and quiet.

"In a similar way, what makes it so special was that when we first got to know each other, we were older than childhood and younger than working. In the winter school communities we each had, there was always a lot of posturing — you remember, cliquishness, role playing. But in the summer — hot, on the lake, without clothes, in the sun, and with no large community to fight against — there was the opportunity, even the demand, for naturalness. There wasn't the usual social pressure to be somebody. Who can you be in the water? Or on a raft in a lake?"

"So it was children, or rather people older than children, in open and useless relationship: to the sun, to the lake, and to each other?"

"Yes. We tied it together with winter vacations there, too. Some of the stories that get retold are winter stories. How coming up one year, Bobby slipped on the icebound lake and broke the bottle of hair tonic in his back pocket. Just as ten years later, when Hank was getting married, Bobby dropped a fifth of Scotch he had been nursing on the train all the way up. Or the time Laurie, Bobby's sister, laughed so hard because of something I said that spaghetti came out of her nose. These moments, that would be totally embarrasing elsewhere, are accepted, even perversely cherished. When Hank telephoned twenty-four girls in a row for a date and no one said yes. And we remember with great fondness that the only reason he telephoned the last ten — it was six o'clock on a Saturday night — was to set a world's record.

"Another tradition was to go, at the end of the summer, to a nearby country club where there was a nine-hole golf course, battered tennis courts — a funky place. It was a tournament among us, very competitive. Except it was not for real, somehow. Nobody could ever decide who won. There were always arguments about it."

"No persona, no facade, no hiding. Everything out in the open." We were both quiet for a moment. "It sounds idyllic." I continued, "a New England pastoral. A *New Yorker* magazine world of nice, privileged kids, not really rich but not too worried, either. With the summer off. Supportive families. Wholesome instincts. Loyalty persisting to the present day."

"Yes. We were lucky. Even privileged, as you say. And we all turned out — so far — pretty well. We've all got our businesses, work for ourselves, and that's unusual these days, more good fortune. Laurie married Hank. She's a schoolteacher. Then there's Kent."

"Why do you sound so sour?"

"Kent disappeared about ten years ago. But he came back for the twentieth reunion: New Year's Day, noon, 1978. He called that morning and wanted to know if it was still on. He said he wasn't going to come because he didn't have any money. Of course I went to pick him up."

Scott's handsome face wrinkled with pain. He noticed that I noticed.

"It was a big high to see him, and then a big low. Kent's a small man, with curly black hair. He said he'd been working nights. The problem for me wasn't that he was poor. The problem was that there was no joy in him. It's hard to explain. It's hard for me to even talk about, because it hurts me when I think about him.

"Kent feels he's not made much of his life. When he came together with us, there was no mirth. We tried to help, like getting him to see his parents for the first time in years. But it didn't work."

Scott paused. "Kent's always missing. We've elected him loser for the summer for the last twelve years, to the point where he is named by acclamation and then we elect someone else, too. We're all angry we can't really include him, angry that we can't help him. We don't know what to do for him."

"Is there other pain involved in the group?"

"Yes. It still serves as a basis for friendship. Two of the people are my real friends, in your sense of the word *friend*. Certainly, with Bobby, I can say anything. We talk long distance on the phone every few weeks. And I try to see Hank when I go to visit my uncle; that's more of a potentially deep friendship, I guess, but it still has something I miss with all the people I've made friends with more recently. With Hank, even when we say nothing, it's richer, deeper, fuller — older and more rooted."

"And the pain?"

"Ah, yes. I have to admit that the group is slowly dissolving. Susan, my wife, is new to the scene. She doesn't enjoy the rites and the traditions. She feels excluded. Even though she likes most of the individuals, the group is not hers. It can never be hers. That undercuts my involvement. And there's less and less time devoted to the group. Nowadays, we only spend a single week, all summer. I have the feeling that may go too, perhaps when the parents start to die. But with Bobby and Hank, I've still got something real, something that goes, I am thankful to say, far, far back."

• • •

Robert Fuller also wanted to be interviewed about friendship, but he is different from Scott Deering. When I arrive at his house, he asks me to sit *in* the hot tub with him while we talk. It is where he likes to spend his leisure hours. Originally from New York, Fuller is now a very Californian psychoanalyst. His curly hair tightens with the steam as we look out over the evening lights of Sausalito, down and across the bay to San Francisco.

He begins with attack. "I am an exception to what you've been finding. I've got friends."

"How old are you?"

"Thirty-nine. It's interesting that you ask, because four years ago I didn't have friends, but Marcia, the woman I live with" — he says it in liberated-man fashion, as if it were one word, *woman-I-live-with,* like *wife* but different — "was always on the phone with her friends, and I finally decided I wanted the same kind of relationship.

"Now, I've got a few friends at various stages of development, but two are really important. Carl lives down there." He gestures toward Sausalito. "He's a carpenter. I'm a big-deal psychoanalyst. I talk about 'transference,' 'narcissism,' and 'libido.' Carl mostly doesn't talk. That's what's good about our friendship. You should meet him. I think he has a number of friends: he's always in the Crosstree Bar and he's always with people. We drink a little bit together, sometimes we play cards. Not much is said but he is important to me.

"Sometimes, when I get too crazy myself, when I get worried or anxious or just start bubbling inside, Carl will see me and say, 'Let's go for a walk.' We go, and he says nothing, but gradually I get the idea that there's a reality outside of what's happening in my head. And I relax. It makes me feel very loved.

"My other friendship is more complex. It's deeper and more important. John Huntington Smith. About my age. He's a surgeon in New York. I've known him for fifteen years, since medical school. He makes five times more money than I do, even though we're both doctors.

"After medical school, we got into a fistfight and didn't see each other for ten years."

This is the first fight I have encountered in my interviews. The old contest between men that unites them in friendship, as at the beginning of Western literature, almost four thousand years ago, between Enkidu and Gilgamesh. It is a bygone rite in our middle-class age, and Robert's mention of it shocks me a little and fills me with curiosity.

"I don't even quite remember myself how the fight started. Some remark John made about my Bohemian ways, as he put it

back then. We had both finished medical school; we were both
married. The wives were present. I clipped him. He clipped me.
The women screamed, and that was the end.

"Until five years ago. One night, he called from New York.
His wife had been killed in an automobile accident, a sudden,
terrible thing. He asked me to come and talk to him. He would
send me a ticket. I told him to keep the ticket and went. So we
talked and we cried together. Then he came out for a week, a few
months after her death, and we sat in the tub. He drank Scotch and
I smoked dope and we just looked at San Francisco.

"Ever since then we see each other. Sometimes he will fly out
at Christmas; last year we met and went skiing in Colorado with
my lady and the woman he's seeing."

I want to go deeper and I press him: "What makes this relationship so special; why do you want to talk about it?"

"As a psychiatrist and as a person, I would say the most important aspect of making a friendship is getting down. It's hard to get
men down. They want to stay on top, to avoid feelings, to avoid
confrontation. They want to stay rational, professional, protected,
and important. In analytic terms, they are afraid of the unconscious — the things that are never said, barely thought, the
shadows that haunt, the jealousies, the yearnings for depth. They
are afraid to love."

I am a little disappointed: this is eloquent and tough, but
Robert sounds like a teacher, rather abstract.

Frustrated, I ask, "So what does that have to do with you and
John?"

"Well, I have insisted that John and I get down. And we have.
I put him in the hot tub and make him relax. I make him take off
his J. Press important doctor suit, the rep tie, the whole bit. I even
get him to take a joint now and then."

"And then?"

"And then we talk. We fight a lot. I like John. I even love John.
And it pisses me off that he's so afraid to be himself. He'll fuck his

girl friend, but he won't live with her. He'll drink Scotch but he won't smoke pot, except occasionally. He doesn't want to look at himself. He wants to keep his middle-class values and his whole trip, but, of course, he's also looking for something deeper. I learned years ago that the most important step with a man is to get beyond the level of friendship where you think you're intimate because you talk about women. You've got to get beyond talking about women. You've got to talk about yourself, about the other guy; above all, you've got to be willing to talk about the relationship.

"So, if something's bothering you, you've got to say it. That means taking a risk — you risk that the other one will go away. We men are, with great reluctance, sometimes willing to do this with our women. We fear that they will go away but we are willing to really have it out, at least occasionally, just because life with some-body close becomes unbearable unless you have it out. Of course, it's safer with women, because generally you've got some kind of agreement going, some kind of formal understanding. It's usually understood with a woman that you are having it out in order to get back in; you're trying to make things better.

"With men, however, there are no models for this. But you've got to do it anyway. You've got to say your say and wait. Moments of fear. Moments of guilt. Until the other reacts. And then you're not sure whether he's right or not. And you have to be willing to show him — a man — your uncertainty, if you're going to be at all honest. You have to let yourself be wounded. You have to get yourself to fight back, if that's right. And again, and again, and again."

Impressed, frightened a little by the hard tasks he demands, I ask him with a new respect, "What do you and John talk about when you have these confrontations?"

"Everything. But it's usually about his being a conformist and afraid to be himself. I think it takes a lot of individuation, an overcoming of the fear of the mother, to be a man, to be oneself, and to be a good friend. I generally drag him into these discussions."

"I don't get it," I protest. "It sounds all one way. You telling John what's what."

Robert smiles. "Did I give that impression? How interesting! Yes, I lay it on — about the horn-rimmed glasses, the woman friend, the private school for the kids, the whole bit. But he's not silent. After a few drinks, he comes back at his friend, 'the big-mouth California psychiatrist,' as he calls me. 'What's bothering you so much, Robert? Why are you so concerned with how much money I make? Why are you pushing so hard on my style of living, Robert? Are you not so sure as you pretend to be about your California bullshit?' That's the way it went last time. 'Your fucking hot tub and hash and your girl friend you won't marry. Why do you have to prove you're right?'

"It's elementary, really, that he catches me so, and naturally he's partly right. And it's not always the same; we don't always fight. But I think it is because we can fight, because we will both risk ourselves and the whole relationship, that we are such good friends. It's time-consuming, it's exhausting, it's exhilarating and a pain in the ass. But for me, it's essential."

• • •

Lambert de Boulonge lives in Belgium, where the air is hardly ever warm, unlike California. The sky is not clear but rather hangs heavy, low, and cloudy over the earth. The *drip, drip* of slow cold rain is nearly constant, in all seasons. It is the kind of country where human comforts and consolations are soberly cherished.

In the dark but well-kept woods, the yellow earth is already a little muddy with the morning rain as I follow Lambert on his rounds. He is a tall man, even a little gangly. The brownish skin is already spotted with age, though he says he is only in his early sixties. He seems worn. He describes himself with a modest shrug as a member of "the bourgeoisie, the *petite noblesse,* if you like."

He stalks ahead of me, his dark green rubber boots softly slapping the wet earth, his right arm swinging his balance, his left arm carrying the long saw with which he trims his trees. Indeed, apart from some investments abroad, they are his living, for he sells lumber and firewood from them.

"I am a countryman. I suppose I would have been some sort of scientist, but when I was at the university I got some goddamned disease. It damaged me for city living and sedentary mental work. So I ended up tending the family woods."

The *drip, drip* continues as we make our way back to the house. Lambert has spent the morning trimming his trees, stacking the wood, his breath rough when he bends, his tall body straining to lift the cut boughs and stack them, and then the long-legged march to the next tree that needs his care. There is a kind of mute dignity about the man. In his old brown woolen coat he has some of the stolid strength of the trees themselves.

"You were going to tell me about your friend Henri," I remind him. We are sitting now in the living room. The furniture, as is so often true in Belgian houses, is old, grand, and too big. Enormous wooden antiques are passed down through old noble families who lived in châteaux too expensive to maintain today. Outside, the *drip, drip* can be heard slipping off the slate roof and falling to the ground. He sits silent, as though his thoughts were lost in the forest. I see that I will have to prompt Lambert; he will give no facile responses, this man.

"You said that Henri and you were real friends. Had you known him a very long time?"

He takes the small black pipe from his mouth. "We had known each other — in a way — for ten years. Because of the music. Each of us was a member of a small chamber orchestra. During the autumn and winter we would get together once a week. Nothing special, you understand; just to practice, just amateurs. In the town up the road, Arles l'Envoi. And so we had been acquaintances, you might say, all that time. But we didn't become friends until four years ago."

The same thoughtful look, the pale blue eyes big with reflection. "Oh, just one of those things — we had a concert the next night. I went to town for the rehearsal, and he asked me if I wanted to stay over instead of driving home. The next day was a Saturday, his wife and children were away, and we talked. And that was how we became friends. After that, we talked often. I would go there, or he would come out here and we would talk in the woods."

"What did you talk about, what made the friendship so important to you?"

"We talked about everything, I suppose." He hesitates.

"Was there some particularly important topic?"

"At our age, we could talk about the important things." He puffs on the pipe now. "We talked about what life was all about. He was a very religious man, in his way, was Henri. So am I. Not in a conventional fashion, you understand, churchgoing and all that; something more personal. We talked a lot about getting older. About losing our powers of mind and body, the horror of maybe having to be dependent, one day, on others. We talked about death."

The *drip, drip* underscores what follows.

"And then?"

"And then Henri got sick. Three years ago he got cancer."

"Were you around when he died?"

"I went to the hospital every day, sometimes two and three times. I was there when he died. I saw his coffin buried."

"Do you think of him?"

"Often. On his last day, I was there with his youngest daughter. She had had a lot of problems — boys, school. He could hardly move his hands, but he motioned us as if to put two things together. He looked at each of us. So she comes to see me a lot and I look after her, give her advice, help however I can. So it continues. I miss him."

The rain continues. Lambert smokes his pipe in silence. I rest content with what he has given me.

• • •

In my own quest, these men and a few others like them seemed to embody important values. In each of their stories there was a certain tenderness, a human valuing of a few close relationships, each with its own authenticity.

Moreover, though they and their friendships were never, to my mind, reducible to simple moral lessons or to abstract insights, they each led me to particular ideas that I thought might be useful in my later searching.

With Scott I saw the special value of comradeships maintained from childhood or youth: a playful current that could be continued into adult life. I was too polite with him: I wanted to but didn't shout, "Hold on! Don't let it go! Keep up the reunions, in some way, even if the parents die; even though you live in different parts of the country, even if your wife doesn't like them or fit in. Above all, don't let go of the two men with whom you feel a special friendship." I wanted Scott to keep the childish quality of sunshine playfulness and to find a way to make those two friendships have ever more grown-up dimensions. A hard task.

A lot of what Robert Fuller said, despite his occasional pomposity, seemed to be true. For deep friendship, it would be necessary to "get down" — to be free to discuss the relationship, to take the risk, to show the shadow side of one's own character and allow the other the same. While I was not, personally, likely to be quite so aggressive and feisty, I knew that friendship might well have to pass through such emotional fires. It seemed part of the truth, at least for certain kinds of relationships. Frequently, friendship is represented as something too steadily pleasant, or in certain of the masterpieces of the past — Aristotle and Cicero, for example — as pervaded by a constant mutual understanding and a gentle calm. Being a psychoanalyst, Robert was an expert on emotion, and I agreed with him that friendship is also an emotional relationship, with involvement that can get hot at times, like any other deep involvement with a person. Achilles' rage, David's mourning over Jonathan: deep emotion is part of the possibility of male friendship and of its tradition.

Lambert, I felt for. He was one of several men I met who showed that new friendships can be formed in adult life and — much more exceptionally — attain a real depth. His friendship of old age was characterized by a wise texture, a truly philosophic content, and in his loyalty to the dead friend's daughter, a force that enables it to live beyond the grave.

I frankly envied each of these men their friendships. They gave me hope. They helped me to believe that I was not crazy to persist.

5

Torment and
a Declaration

Over a two-year period my personal quest had not brought me much. Not that all my attention focused on male frendship. During this period I met Jacqueline and married her. She loyally supported my quest for friendship — at first, simply because it was mine, and later, as we talked more and more about the critical issues involved, with acute comprehension. It was she who suggested we move to her home in Brussels, at the very center of Western Europe. I needed time to think, to become more and more focused on friendship and to write about it. Moreover, I imagined that Europe should have something to teach Americans about friendship.

In the relative isolation of an alien culture, despite my foreign languages and my European literary education, the quest deepened. With an inevitability that can only come from isolation and, eventually, homesickness, I let myself sink into my subject with increasing single-mindedness. I let myself pursue friendship with an attentive heart and a careful eye, noting what I saw around me and in me, both.

. . .

After the first few weeks of appreciating the novelty of my Belgian surroundings, I discovered the inner toll the first two years had taken. One night, we entertained a pleasant, tall, distinguished-looking man: a dark, fortyish professor of sociology at the University of Louvain — intelligent, sensitive, even, as the Belgians say, "charming." I warmed to him and his interesting conversation and thought, as he left after dinner, that perhaps here could be a new friend. But the following morning I wrote:

A Year and Six Months After the Lunch with Harry Solano

What is it? What is it that bothers?

Something familiar. A lightness, perhaps, in this professor. Too much lightness like Harry Solano? Too soft a man in the end? Too charming like Ronald Sutherland?

Or is it something that has no relation to him, or even to the type of man he or others may be? Perhaps something more general. Something within me that says, "Not so open. Don't be too eager. Don't get burned again."

This is a new inner voice: caution. I am surprised to hear it. Usually I am eager, I lean into new experience. Suddenly I am calculating in spite of myself. I am, indeed, rightly calculating. I know now, again and alas, how hard it is to make a new attachment that will not hurt.

Am I dying to friendship again? "Twice dead?" An anti-heroic parody of mysticism's twice born? Or is it simply prudence — the kind old Cicero recommends in *De Amicitia*? Whichever or both, I do not like what is happening.

My inner voice made me aware that I had caught myself in the very act: the unconscious process of self-defending we have all been through in our twenties and thirties as the friends of our youth slip away and other, new connections fail. This is the persistently growing armor of age, and I have to struggle to keep it off if I am to stay alive to new possibilities of friendship.

After some months in Europe, without my thinking about it, my heart naturally turns homeward to people in America I have known for years, men and women both, whom I had not been able to bring closer to me that first year of trying. Despite travel, despite research, despite family life, I am being pressed by my isolation and my needs for contact. At a distance, I am able to see these old acquaintances more clearly and more fondly. Indeed, there has never been any lack of fondness; rather, a lack of our engaging deeply with one another.

On some days then my heart can open to the old people in my life, and there are moments of intense revelation and sweetness.

After Three Months in Europe

Months now away from my old American friends. Months in which my relationships with them have been carried on with a premeditation impossible in person.

I have had that distance my French-speaking acquaintances call *le recul*. It has allowed my relationships to come alive for me as subjects of contemplation. Not as coldly intellectual and distant subjects but rather as vividly imagined realities, ones on which my feelings have played in the mind for stretches of hours. Where with that mental focus letter writing allows, I have held four or five of my old friends in my heart.

In some instances, we have worked together, sharing the pleasure of joint achievements, suffering the failure of disappointed projects. Then, after we have each moved on to new work, we have remained occasional confidants to one another, sympathetic participants in personal struggles. We have come — bidden by spouses — to one another's birthday parties, invited one another to Christmas celebrations when, at various times, each has needed a place to go for the lonesome American holidays. We have helped one another get jobs, listened to complaints about bosses, understood with nodding heads the agonies of living in difficult couples; even, on occasion, helped analyze one another's dreams. Thus we have been more than colleagues, more than comrades, much more than mere acquaintances or pals, and yet not all that friends would truly mean.

As the recently arrived foreigner, I am isolated from deep personal intercourse with the new people around me. So I cherish my distant friends much more than if we were close. Sitting down alone, day after day, I summon each in my imagination, letting each live within me as I hold him steady in memory and fantasy and write long, thoughtful letters.

Beautiful letters, I try to make them: gifts full of frankness, of interesting observations, of caring.

These long, personal letters permit a peculiarly intensified relating. With no one really there to respond, one person must do the work of two, conjure the relationship — past and present — into being for two.

Thus, you in California or New York or Connecticut, I have held in my mind. I have seen you thousands of miles away. I have had to clothe airy nothingness with the fabrics of the imagination, to give your distant being imminent flesh. I have colored your faraway cheeks with blood and remembered with a minute attention and care the color of your hair, the luminosity of your eyes, the crow's feet beginning to form. Here, far away, in cloudy Belgium I have done all this.

So I realize I have taken you and hung your images in my heart, like the treasured icons in a church. Indeed, it is not too much to say that this physical separation, and my will to break it, has led to a cherishing, a habit of endearment, that resembles worship. Not the worship of the divine, but of lesser beings charged with what one perceives as divine qualities of goodness, of substantiality. In all my lonesome hours before the blank pages of correspondence, you have become to me a family of phantoms rich with benevolence, people I have learned to love more fully in absence. An inner family I have reached for and held and, by this sheer act of willed contemplation, drawn mysteriously closer to me than, probably, had been likely had we merely been together in the old and usual ways.

I have been strangely confident that this was no mere solipsistic fancy. That I was not only fantasizing but, rather, developing in fact the intensity of what actually is between us, an intensity we ignore when we are together — whether out of shyness or uncertainty, or the contemporary prejudice against taking friendship really seriously.

It is, above all, the letters that have done this. My careful letters. You have not been, no one can be, immune to those palpable proofs, deposits from the spirit world like so much ectoplasm, of my existence and my care for you. Those letters have arrived in your busy American lives — distracted, jangly, media-awash world — like reminders of another time, eighteenth- or nineteenth-century anachronisms full of the sincerity, the contemplativeness, and the honoring of personality of a more leisured time. Startling, wonderful. Difficult for you.

One of you has said that I write "a good nineteenth-century letter, full of reflectiveness and circumstantiality." The wording of the description contains a kind of soft protest. How, after all, is he to respond? How is his Manhattan life to be reconciled with this sepia print taken a week ago in Europe and forwarded mysteriously out of time, by nothing less than air mail?

This friend protests — as have the rest of you in mute ways — that I call you from excessive modern wakefulness back to the inner dreaminess of reality. You resist writing letters as do all modern people. You are afraid to commit yourselves, even to the page. You cherish the freedom to be spontaneous, to telephone. Instantaneous you. But there I am, waiting for a response, handwritten, my being evoked by every inky letter on each piece of thin stationery.

So, now, you are compelled to imagine *me*: a Stuart who is not only the writer of the letter but who is also your Stuart. I tease you with the paradox of the double Stuart of these letters: implied flesh and blood that covers paper with plastic ink, a real being, out there over the ocean; also a clear fiction, the creation of your mind. You realize that my marks on paper are but symbols, words that stand for a presence which you must summon, like a spirit, like a witness.

If you refuse this work at first and read the letter hurriedly once, then thrust it away, it cannot be fully put off. It lies heavy in your pocket. Mysteriously, as time passes, the letter occupies an ever larger space in the pile on your desk. It recalls me to you. It calls you to remember me. It calls you, as ever more time slips by, to imagine what I am like now, what changes I have suffered since I wrote, so long ago. Ironically, the longer you delay writing me, the bigger place I occupy in your consciousness.

And so, when you force yourself against all present habits to respond, to write, then, at last, *you* must hold me with the same willed clarity and deliberation in your own imagination as I have you. Now must *you* create a whole new scene, with just the two of us in it. You must bridge worlds, rolling Belgian clouds and California sunshine together, your shorts and tanned legs and my throat, scarf-wrapped against the cold.

Each time I receive your letter, even if sometimes brief and noncommittal, I know I have gotten inside you. Beyond any intimate whispering in your ear — a closeness, in any case, never likely these arms-off days — closer than the depths of your body, I have crept into your mind.

To realize the importance the imagination could have in friendship, to understand its immense power for bringing us together in a way, to feel my inner attitudes toward my American friends deepening — all this was at once a significant discovery and a comfort. An Austrian novelist I met and with whom I discussed this said, "Of course! In fact, we always exist for one another *only* in our separate imaginations."

Profoundly true; but not entirely enough for me. After all, one wants the more tangible communication also.

Recklessly, perhaps bravely, I let myself grow full of wanting — wanting simple, real friendship. I told only Jacqueline about this growing intensity; I felt it would frighten friends away. I acknowledged this part of my aloneness, my forlornness, more and more in my heart. I dwelt on it despite the dangers of renewed disapointment.

One of the friends from America, perhaps the dearest to me in my silent, private experience, was spending the summer in Spain. I took the chance, charged as I was with the knowledge of my yearning, of responding to Wreston's invitation to visit. The journal entry that follows reflects, in its relative incoherence, the intensity I was allowing myself to feel.

I believe this intensity is latent in many of us; each one of us holds our own particular version of it. It is an intensity that is the repressed reciprocal of our well-known modern diseases: loneliness, boredom, insecurity. It is the intensity of our real but hidden friendlessness. Intensity and some incoherence are part of the search for real friendship.

After Four Months in Europe

A long time since I have written in this journal. It has been a difficult time. But then something happens like the visit to Wreston and I take courage.

Wreston the difficult, Wreston the irascible. Wreston the

angry. I often wonder why I put up with him. Of course, the simple answer is that I love him. Not because he is funny, though that, too, is part of it. Not even because he makes me feel, sometimes, that life can be lived with extreme dangerousness. But because I love him. Surely, that is enough.

Wreston has gotten older. His hair is turning white in his late fifties. A lot of mileage on that particular life — childhood in the streets, a famous sculptor, the Whitney Museum and all that. Now, largely forgotten. Still banging away on his own, "scraping by in every sense," as he likes to say.

His wit can be light and easy or hard and sharp like his chisel. Despite some recent generosities, I never know when he will be mean to me, so deep runs his irritation. Once in the Seattle airport, three years ago, after a misunderstanding between us, he hurt me so much with what he said about me, indicting my very being, that we didn't speak for two years. He had tears running down my cheeks. That was the worst time of my whole life, packed with personal disaster, but it would be the time when Wreston would choose to let go.

Yesterday I rode toward him on a narrow highway, for hours, through Spanish drizzle. Miles on miles of tall bent grass and wet sheep. The house, when Jacqueline and I arrive, is small, dreary, and cold. Wreston's family, as often, is tense. Wreston turned from the small stove, skillet in hand, and irritably asked his young wife to change the crying baby. In the scattered room diapers, old plates, American magazines, some miscellaneous chips from statues brought in by the baby from the studio. The couple came here to get away from Seattle's drizzle for a few months and it is not working well. Wreston's wife was trying to stay calm. Against all odds, she was trying to read the final pages of Thomas Mann's *The Magic Mountain*. Everybody was irritated by the strangeness of the season. Here it was July and still cold and raining.

Over the first few hours, Wreston was particularly

standoffish. Wrapped in himself. His moodiness I have come to expect and dread. Night passed into day and Wreston asked me to go with him to gather wood — abandoned fence, twigs, old construction materials.

"Is this piece of land yours also?" I asked.

"It belongs to the sonofabitch farmer who sold me my house and then tried to cheat me of a room — can you believe that, he tried to pretend that one of the rooms wasn't part of the deal. So I take his wood to fuck him over."

It was one of several dozen irascible signs he had given me that he was especially full of anger and hatred. From the first hours of my visit I had told myself that I had best develop all the inward restraint I could. I was not going to have amusement, camaraderie, or even a normally empty and pleasant social time here. And as for the closeness of friendship — forget it. He had even started criticizing Jacqueline. But she and I both knew it best to say nothing. Even though that invited further attack. Wreston's pain was so raw, an irritability so naked, as to drive him out of ordinary restraints and expectations. Jacqueline and I were both a little afraid of him.

He ripped away at a dead tree root. His face still tugging with his arms, he turned an eye to me, dropped the root, looked, and said very directly and simply, suddenly defenseless, "I've been strangely anxious lately. I've had a very hard time sleeping. Do you have some tranquilizers or sleeping pills on you? I can't get anything here, don't know enough Spanish."

Strange to say, but it made the whole long trip from Belgium worthwhile. All the miles of wretched country, rain, and disappointment.

I've already said I love him.

There are not four people in the whole round world that he would ever — paranoid, angry, defensive, proud — ever ask for that kind of help. His wife, a sister, and now me. It was a confession so simple and direct of his current weakness: "I am weak, help me!" This unbending creature, who preferred the solitary independence of cheap cafeterias to being served in restaurants (so great was his distaste at asking for anything). But he asked me.

In his question was focused a whole relationship. Of course, I was concerned about what was bothering him, though I knew enough to ask nothing about it, at least not yet. But there was, in his reaching out to me, an immediate and shared transcendence of that pain. Not only that pain but the ordinary human pain of separation that we both suffer every day. That Wreston would trust me with his most mundane weakness, heroic he who liked to make his statues scream anguish as big as gods and to represent himself as a tormented Prometheus who would joke about his pain but never cry. That he would simply ask for a goddamned pill to pop him off to sleep, so, was fearfully, ridiculously, gloriously intimate.

In his proud way he let me see him on his knees. The steel that seemed to separate us and that separates me from other men — and often women, too — was suddenly as weak and soft as a shoji panel in a Japanese screen. His pushing through it implied everything we shared, everything on which he could base his trusting: the same torture from sensitive feelings and bodies. The same exhaustion, as if much of every day was lived on the high wire. The same what? The same whatever that made us, tenuously, friends. Even though in this peculiar age we didn't live nearby, we didn't see each other much, and we weren't even sure the other really cared. But, I know I love him, and in that moment, he broke through to say, without saying, that he thought I probably did and he could be, with me, simply himself.

When, later, I gave Wreston the five pills, the moment had already past. There is nothing very poetic about pharmaceuticals. I could see that even though I had hidden the transfer from both our wives, there was some other audience in his own mind who despised him for asking for and resorting to

Swiss happy powders. Still, the moment had focused an understanding. We had known each other, off and on, for twelve years. Perhaps the event even implied that we would continue and deepen our relationship led on two continents, that there would be no more dropping one another for years of silence, that we would continue to be friends. Though we both knew our world was empty of such assurances, still, as I say, his request was worth the whole trip.

Two Days Later

It doesn't happen every day, but I have had to fight today and many times before the thought that there is something wrong with me to care so much about friendship and even to be so conscious of the caring. I look at my experience with Wreston. I see my wanting a deep alliance with him and I feel ashamed. I see myself joyful because we have had, after years of acquaintance, a moment of trust and engagement, and I feel, again, that I have betrayed my manliness to be so excited, especially about such a little gesture.

I have to defend myself to myself. I must assert what is obviously true but hard to remember, that to want friends is not aberrant. I am simply responding to the ancient but living ideal of male friendship. It is still alive in our culture, if in great measure merely as an ideal. And I have to assert that not to have the deep friendships I want is only partially my personal fault. For what human relationship is intact nowadays? Where is the student and the teacher? Where is the boss and the worker? Where, even, is the husband and the wife? I must fight the idea that there is something wrong with me to care about this. Painful though it is, I must keep looking.

Two Months After the Trip to Spain

It is merely my imagination that my letters matter, and it is more. I imagine my friendships and they really advance in depth. This morning at last a letter from Wreston:

Dear Stuart,

I'm sorry I won't be seeing you for so long. I look forward to the next time very much. You're one of the very very few people I have known whose presence delights me and makes me happy. You can catch any ball I can throw.

It must have been something of a drag for you to see me in Spain, when I was in the middle of an acute crisis, the worst I have experienced in memory. Maybe someday I'll tell you all about it. My state of mind is somewhat better now, though I do exist in a state of suspended or controlled despair. As you know so well, I'm fundamentally a high-wire man, and if the gauge of my wire is changed, ever so slightly, I feel that my life is in terrible danger, that I will fall into the void.

I will write to you again.

I love you a lot and I hope that from time to time I have indicated this (in my own slanty way of course).

Love,
W.

I was totally surprised. Not so much at what he said — the content — but that he had said it in the first place.

I have known Wreston twelve years in a typical, modern American friendship. We first met in New York; I was consulting for an art school where he taught. His tight, stringy presence, his wit, his dark gray courage to say whatever he thought and to face his own pain — all that made me love him at once. I loved his angry hammering at the stone from which he made his statues. Then his meditated stroking the emerging curves. He picked them out with his chisel, rubbed them down with his sandpaper, carefully blew the dust away to ponder the line. We had coffee and lunch and dinner — four days running. Then I got back on a plane to California. A typical American friendship.

Except for another brief visit to New York, I didn't hear from Wreston for six years. We were again instant comrades, in Berkeley this time. He and his first wife had divorced, he had left his teaching job, and he was wandering the earth for a place. We prowled the streets, one early middle-aged man and one late middle-aged man, joking and laughing like undergraduates, looking at the coeds with joyful lust, playing verbal games with one another. After a few weeks, he was off again. This time to Seattle to open his own art school, then to Europe for the summers. In the next six years he married a second time and had a son. We only saw each other five times, the last time two months ago in Spain.

Not much to base a friendship on, really: intense rapport but not much time together. Vast reservoirs of confidences, especially on his unbending side, kept to oneself. Though his appearance betrays his intense nervousness and willingness to be different, he keeps himself tight with other secrets, which, I imagine, no one knows. He is the taut high wire of which he now writes me.

This letter from him puts our friendship on a new footing, in a way. It is all that was implied in the asking for the drugs back in Spain, but, by being an outright declaration, it subtly changes matters, makes them stronger between us.

Not that I have any illusions. The man is stretched very thin, especially now. He needs my help and I will try to give it — long distance and by letter as I can. I shall write him often; if he wants, I will fly back to the States for him. But there is no point in thinking too much about it, much less actually going, unless he asks. How can I expect him to ask when he hasn't even told me what it is that torments him?

Despite Wreston's confession of love, his reserve continues. Being the kind of creature he is, he shrinks from touch like a wild dog. I know not to ask too much of him. Even that I offer to help him.

Our friendship is not all that I want, but it is more than I have had.

Wreston was a real comfort to me, alone as I was in ever-more-rainy Belgium.

But when my life got tougher, I turned, by mail, to another American.

6

Unreason and
a Call for Help

Irrationality is a largely unexplored side of friendship, particularly in modern times. True friends would be there for one another when the going gets hard, hard not only in a material way but, more usually these days, in an emotional way.

There are some contented, well-adjusted, well-balanced types in the world; and there are rigid, blindered, careful types in the world. Both escape a lot of the pain of living.

Most people these days have their inner struggles, at least from time to time, and moments when life seems hard, even unbearable. Indeed, this wrestling with ourselves is a central theme of modern literature and art. In this connection, I always like to recall an interview with Isaac Bashevis Singer shortly after he had received the Nobel Prize. Without any apparent motive, the interviewer asked the old man who had now become about as successful as a writer could become, "Do you ever think about suicide?" Singer replied, "Often, of course. What can you think about all day — potato pancakes?"

Without romanticizing our problems, we must admit that deep strain is part of life. We are foolish and expect ourselves to be wholly reasonable, even though from time to time the fit can take us. The fit of worry, anxiety, and depression took me, in Europe, largely alone, committed to an awareness of my aloneness, oppressed by midlife Weltschmerz and unchanging gray skies. Who knows why it took me? If we really understood our irrationality, there would be no need for hundreds of competing schools of psychology.

I plunged into despondency. My wife tried but couldn't wholly help. Now, I truly needed a close man friend. Need was beyond mere want.

A Month After Wreston's Letter

I seem, sometimes, to keep track of my relationships as other men keep track of the stock market.

Probably for the same motive.

The illusions of safety. Some men clutch their stock reports the way I clutch letters from home — in the hope that they will make me feel less desolate.

On days when reality mysteriously vanishes and anxiety and fear take its place, pain gnashes the teeth and everything oppresses — the latest maneuvers of the Red Army on television are laden with personal danger; a refugee's face is mine; an insolent bus driver seems momentarily as authoritative and powerful as a prison guard. Worry fills the mind — about money, about health, about success. About our appalling ignorance. What do we know to do about the Russians? About famine? Even about inflation?

Bad days like this, I desperately want to talk to a friend. As the whirlpool sucks me downward, I want to reach up an arm. Take hold! Hold me! Pull! At the very least, help me remember who I am. That I am a person who can carry on, not overwhelmed by petty worries or cosmic. That I know what I am doing, what life is about. That I am Stuart, the fellow who occupies my skin.

Two Days Later

A downward driving gloom has taken me and I am scared.

I am scared it will continue, as it has at times, for weeks. It seems to come of itself. A fear creeps onto my heart and begins to work its teeth like a dog tearing, soon as I wake up each morning.

I know that I have what psychologists call, nowadays, depression. That simple and ordinary. Many people get depressed. In the Renaissance they called it melancholia. Before that, who knows? Who cares?

I do. I hope to find a rationale for these feelings — to know that they are, in some sense, all right, normal, typical, ancient, human. Knowing that people have always felt this way, some of the time, is no comfort to me. That only makes it worse.

Jacqueline takes my fears on. Each worry at a time.

"It will be all right.

"We have enough money.

"What can we do if the Russians come? We'll cope like everyone else.

"It won't last forever; you know you'll feel better after a while. Don't worry."

With wifely patience, day by day, she speaks to cheer me up and to reweave each fiber of preoccupation into some whole fabric of my ordinary self. I try to help her. Sometimes, for hours or days at a time, it is enough. But generally, it is not enough.

I need men friends. My relationships, such as they are, become very important. I will reach toward you, fellow men. I need you. To be strong and remind me of who I am. I don't even know what I am asking for, exactly. The wife alone is not enough. Good as she is. No one person is enough. Perhaps your male strength is what I need.

Next Day

I have written to Bob Jones about my depression. Why I have picked Bob to write to in this moment I am not sure. Despite our being in the same social circles for many years, I don't know him very well. Nor do I feel with Bob the deep kinship I have with Wreston. There is often pain and a rage in Wreston that is, despite our different styles, somehow like my own. I know that Wreston would understand what I am feeling.

Logically, I should have written to him. I turn, instead, to Jones. Wreston might well understand but he is in crisis himself. Perhaps, given his stronger nature, his pain is greater than mine. Frankly, I do not think he can handle me at this point. My depths of raw sewage will only disgust him further, with me and with himself.

Bob Jones is another sort of person. Bob Jones has broad shoulders and a steady, clear, and blue-eyed gaze. Bob Jones wears steel-rimmed glasses at one extremity and Wallabees at the other. Bob Jones keeps his two foreign cars clean, inside and out. Wreston's old heap is filthy, full of crud, baby's milk turned to cheese in the secret crevices of back seats. Jones wears honest, plaid, button-down shirts, and Jones has an honest button-down family: handsome boys, blond as flax, blue jeans Rinso-bright, big comfortable faces. Bob Jones has been married for nearly thirty years to the same faithful person, who wears her red hair tightly curled.

If anyone will help, it is Bob Jones.

But can Bob help? To help he must first understand. Reliable as a Maine garage mechanic, thoughtful, pure, and good, can he possibly understand the early winter craziness I know is illusory but that still frightens — all the worries in the world from Russians and work and money to advancing age?

Probably, possibly.

After all, Bob is crazy too. He's not totally square. He gave up a professorship to lead a more open, searching life. Seven years ago, Bob spent a year staring at tidepools, noting their changes from dawn to night through the seasons of the year. He wrote a book. What matter if his country woodpile is stacked as neatly as a Bavarian peasant's or that his cars are as clean as a plate? He has studied psychology! He has been in therapy!

In fact, I am not sure of Bob.

It may presume too much on our nascent friendship to dump my pain on him. Though we had known of each other through mutual acquaintances for years, we have only met a dozen times, all during the last two years. True, I did Bob a big favor once. There's a debt I can call on there. On the other hand, despite a certain generic sympathy I feel for him and he for me, I sense Bob is too reserved to leap into anything resembling real emotions. He may think me dangerous — worse, ridiculous. I may turn him off, entirely.

But I remember Bob's sitting over coffee the first time we met. We talked about friendship. The lack of it.

"Yes, now that I think about it, I don't have real friends in that sense. I guess I've known for a long while. My wife has a few close friends. Sometimes she nags me about it. As if all one had to do was pick up the phone! She doesn't understand that men can't do that." Bob had looked at me, very briefly, full of puzzled resignation.

I had liked the candid admission of friendlessness. I appreciated his understanding of the trapped pathos of our inept manliness, with no ready ways of reaching out. Perhaps there was too much stoicism, too much acceptance of our plight. But I will gamble on Bob's depth.

Two Weeks After Writing to Bob Jones

I knew that Jones would reply promptly.

> Dear Stuart,
>
> Your dark and painful letter arrived yesterday, and I'm trying to answer quickly even though I realize that by the time you get it your mood may be very different. I hope so, of course, although I wish that there were some way for

you to wrestle with that particular angel and win its bless-
ing before you chase it away. (Genesis 32:24–31 — it's
hell to have to give citations in a personal letter!) As you
say, this darkness is old stuff for you, and I suppose that it'll
keep up the return visits, like some old unwanted maiden
aunt, until . . . until . . . shit, I don't know! Until you guess
its name, I suppose. It's hard to know how to talk about it
across so many miles, although I'd be hard pressed to be
very helpful even if you were three feet away. Let me just
ramble for a little . . .

I'm moved by your honesty and openness with me. I'm
also struck with how important the privacy issue is in this
matter — your telling me to discuss your letter with no one,
not my wife, nor the other people we both know. Of
course, I will accede to your wishes. But I wonder, why all
the secrecy? People know you back here. Are you afraid
they will say, 'He was so happy last spring when he decided
to kick off his job, go to Europe, and just write. It all
seemed a little too jubilant, at the time. Just goes to show
you.' Well, people might say that, might think it. I think it a
bit myself. And so what? I was puzzled by your inexplicable
happiness last spring. Frankly, I feel relieved that you're
back on the ground. Even though I wish you were happier
now . . .

I do sympathize with and worry about you. I don't have
any answers. I have a lot of concern, and I'll be anxious to
hear from you whenever you want to talk.

I think as I finish, that's pretty good, as far as it goes. My
letter was a hard one to respond to at all.

I *judge* Bob's response. Despite the real pain with which I
wrote him, I judge his response. My letter about the pain was
at once heartfelt and also a kind of test. I am testing who he is,
testing his ability to respond to my deep needs. Making sure

before I tell him more. Trying to find out at what level we can really be friends, to what degree.

Here I am feeling irrationally overwhelmed. At the same time I draw back to observe how good a job Bob does of trying to save my life. There's something mad about this caution and testing. But it is so.

I am genuinely comforted. A "dark and painful letter" it was, and Bob's words acknowledge that and give my trouble some abstract shape. I am, to some degree, known. Bob has also, by implication of simply seeing who I am, accepted me and my darkness.

That business about wrestling with angels, though, is some kind of humanistic psychology crap. Or Jungian. Or Christian.

What angel?

But I like the "shit I don't know." That seems human. I am grateful for Bob's concern, his frustration.

So far so good. In a general way the risk has paid off. Jones says he can't help me but at least he is willing to try and see me and to say that he's frustrated that he can't help me. That's real. That's comradeship.

There is also a drawing away I had too rightly anticipated from a man who, while acquainted with feelings, keeps his rather carefully out of sight. He exaggerates, for example, the difficulties posed to correspondence by time and space. Yes, it's possible that my "mood" (the word trivializes what I had experienced) has changed; indeed, it is somewhat lighter by the time his letter arrives. But suppose it wasn't? Anyway, I need his direct response to what I wrote, not his fantasy that it may be obsolete to give it. Moreover, "like some old unwanted maiden aunt" makes my pain ridiculous, domesticates it to an archetype of familiar nuisance.

Bob comes toward me and then backs away. I would have wished he had just come forward.

The part of the letter about confidentiality even makes me angry. I have run into the brick wall of his steady conventionality. Out here, in Europe, it is still conventional to keep matters of a personal nature private between people. But in sunny California, everybody, conventionally, "shares," as they say, everything. My desire to confide in him, to create some special alliance between us, to fall on his shoulder only, to show myself in my worst mood only to him, is taken as false. A maneuver to save face for the ego.

Oh, I have known that California sharing — sitting around in groups, whether paid or of "friends," and "spilling your guts," and then feeling the group support, getting the group criticism, imbibing the group's advice. All very fine. Except afterward, you feel as lonely as before, because you have, in fact, gotten only help. You haven't gotten into anyone else's being. Might as well have called a hot line and spoken to some earnest social work trainee. Or paid a therapist for fifty minutes. There's no love there. For love, we've got to be alone, together. We've got to close out everyone else. Bob Jones knows that, of course. Everyone knows that. But he backs away. He accuses me of wanting to present a face to the world instead of what is in fact so — wanting to be with him.

No, he is not going to be easily drawn in, old Bob.

The letter continues. It shifts and turns to fill out a page and a half of dense typewriting. It leaves me at the end with uncertainty. I'm not sure to what extent Bob is trying to be helpful or simply trying to appear helpful. Probably a little of both. His care to keep his *own* feet on the "ground" is quietly enraging to me.

The Next Day

What a confused coming and going of feelings I've had in regard to Bob's letter. Appreciation and gratitude, resentment, contempt, even rage.

And as I read and reread his letter I am less and less sure which of these feelings are appropriate. Perhaps I am too harsh: what I take for evasion may only be Bob's desperate attempts to say *something*, anything, in reply to a painful letter from a friend far away. Perhaps he is right about last spring. My euphoria was merely a mood and not, as I had thought, a deeper feeling based on an unprecedented inner certainty of my place in the world. Then, I had summoned the courage to cut off my supports, to strike out on my own into an uncertain future. Perhaps it was only a kind of false hope. But I had wanted Bob to recall my courage, not tell me it was a delusion. I had wanted him to say, "Be calm, go on, I too saw who you were, and you *can* make it on your own terms." Only now do I understand what I wanted from him — that affirmation. I should have told him so. But, if I had, he would have given me the wrong response: as he says in his letter, he didn't believe in my adventure.

Round and round I turn, more and more confused about bubbling, intense feelings.

At last, I take a cowardly way:

"Dear Bob,

"This is only a quick and brief reply to your good letter but I want you to know that I am grateful for your concern and appreciative of your advice: both have helped me . . ."

And so forth. I risk nothing negative. I butter him up, albeit briefly. I reassure him implicitly that his crazy friend is apparently not crazy all the time. I fade out. I push him away, very gently, the way I feel pushed away, not fully engaged. I don't know how else to handle Bob.

Despite his writing and even caring, Jones had disappointed me. Granted his careful nature and the relative shallowness of our acquaintance, it could have been no other way. In my need for friendly understanding and help, I wanted a kind of full response Bob could never give at this stage. I could have, therefore, pulled away from him entirely and taken my sensitive feelings — typical of many men, I think, who don't dare to reach for friendship — wholly into myself. I didn't want to do that anymore: I had a deep need to be known, and I respected very much how Bob Jones had tried — within real and his own self-imposed limits — to be of help.

A Month After My Reply to Bob's Letter

I have been mulling and churning the Bob Jones business for weeks.

I don't like what I did. There's no point in retreating. I can kill our nascent friendship that way. Even though he hurt my feelings by his obtuseness and caution, I am going forward. Today I wrote him a good long letter, but in part I protested.

I don't know you very well. But I resent your psychoanalyzing my request for privacy. I asked for it for several reasons. One was that you wouldn't discuss me with others according to your own partial view. The one that is of least use to me — *that rascal Stuart has gone off again: watch out!* I know that part of you, the cautious, bourgeois, buttoned-up and buttoned-down part of you, is inclined to trivialize my expatriate venture into midlife renewal, my chasing after a Europe that could well be dead, my jumping into total uncertainty by traveling, writing. I know that part of you is inclined to cheapen my great adventure with moralistic interpretation. I know that if you share the fact of my recent "depression" and despair with others you will reinforce yourself in this view of me.

But what I need from you, as my friend, is the other side of your vision. Your sense that all is possible, that risks must be taken, that life can be renewed, and that the future is as likely to bring good things as bad.

That's one reason I want you to keep what I write you private.

The most basic reason, however, is that I want to tell these things, for the moment, only to you. I don't want a crowd listening. I don't want to dissipate the charge of a confidence, a kind of gift from me to you, with a lot of other personalities.

Just you and me, baby.

Besides, since when is it necessary to apologize for wanting privacy?

I decide to make the rest of the letter much milder — some stuff about Europeans vs. Americans. News. I cushion my criticism in the informal neutral, fearing that if I react even slightly tough to this man I know so little, I will put him off forever.

How cautious I have become. Deeply uncertain whether a few frank words of objection might destroy a relationship. As if, nowadays, one has to pick his way with tight-lipped care in our friendless world. Never reveal too much of what you *really* think. Although people will listen and smile to your face, later they will simply cut you off.

I think it quite likely that Jones will say to himself, "Stuart is too difficult. First he asks for help, then he objects to the way I give it. He's in Europe, far away. I'll just forget about him. Plenty of other things to do." Bob will then get up out of his chair, bang his pipe against the brick fireplace, catch the ashes in the cup of his hand, and toss them on the embers of the fire.

I decide to take the risk. I carry my second letter to the post office, but I am worried about it. It is winter, cold and rainy and dark and dreary in Brussels. Not a time to feel alone in the world. I may not love Bob Jones, not yet. But I find much about him likable and very honorable. With the uncertainties in life multiplied by the coming of early evening winter darkness, I *need* people to be there.

The search for friendship, I discover, is complicated by unreason. First the unreason of our own states of being — the crises, the times we fall off center, when we become worried, importunate, anxious. Then, the search is complicated by all the secondary feelings that we develop toward those states of being. One becomes easily ashamed, gun-shy, at once demanding of help and hypercritical of how others react. Other people, we know, can be put off by our being less than our smiling, steady, "normal" selves. They can be additionally put off by our becoming suddenly supersensitive to how they react to our crises.

Of course, if one has real friends, all this back and forth, this approach and avoidance, this careful dancing, doesn't happen. A crisis? Sure. One deals with it confidently, out of experience and trust. However, if one is searching for friends, then events are more uncertain, complex, touchy, and one can reveal only some of what one feels. One would never, for example, reveal envy.

Three Weeks Later

No real word from Jones yet, but his family's Xeroxed Christmas Letter (sounds like some sort of papal message) arrived today along with a few Christmas cards containing brief annual recaps from three other people I know.

Back in America, it seems everybody is depressingly "great" at holiday time.

It's been a good year for Jones and everyone else. Kids are fine, studies have advanced, families are coming together to celebrate, and the New Year looks equally promising.

Jones himself is the worst: this year has been spectacular for him — though, always upright, he doesn't boast. He has published a book, very well reviewed besides. In addition, he's got another scholarly book coming out. *And* he is working on a couple of short stories! Gone at last, he writes, are the long years of quiet contemplation, little work. (He doesn't mention depression or desperation about what to do with his life, states of feeling I know he passed through but that he will refuse to celebrate at this festive season.)

All this recital makes me envious. I am disgusted with myself, even as I fight the Christmas blues, that I am so little identified with my friends that I resent their successes.

Do we share so little as that?

To my own risky letter, no reply, but at the bottom of his encyclical, underneath the six photographs of him, wife, and family, a little handwritten note: "I loved your letter and will write soon. Bob."

It is not a lot, God knows. Not enough to overcome the semiofficial mongering of year-end good cheer, but it is a frail fishline of reality between us. The early stages of an authentic, private exchange, just between me and him.

A Week After Christmas

True blue.

That scribbled note declared he would write and he has.

"As I said in my note on our Christmas letter, I appreciated and liked your letter. I accept your request for privacy and will honor it without further analysis. Much more than that, I appreciate your honesty in explaining what concerns you there."

Bob took my anger about his psychoanalyzing my wish for privacy and accepted it. It is a tad formal, the way he writes, of course. He is cautious with his own feelings. Nevertheless I am glad.

The plunge deeper into the issues that feelings raise for friendship had brought us closer. I had reached out to Bob Jones and he triumphs, my small and pained rejections, my real but thin imagined rapports. All the comings and goings, the eddying efforts toward something real, the tiny melodrama of my struggle against aloneness. All this with the friendship of Richard Stone and the man he lives with.

Stone is a young free-lance filmmaker whom everyone seems to know and regard highly. Asking around in the large English-speaking community here for men to interview about friendship, his name comes up several times. People lower their voices slightly, for such matters are not yet as open as in San Francisco, to confide: "Stone's homosexual." Once more, it is the truly queer and modern association between male friendship and being gay. People also add, "Stone's very clever," which means that he is intellectually gifted.

Today we meet for the first time, and I am interested to observe a large, muscular, young man of pleasant face, thoughtful eyes, and an Anglo-Saxon upper-class laconicism. From what he says about his work, I come to see quickly that Stone's detached manner belies a dedicated working at the problems of the planet. He also has the best personal collection of recorded operas I have ever seen and a large, fascinating library. Strong and self-assured, Richard Stone is a man who seems, despite an occasional boyish gleam of humor, much older than he is.

My own preparations for this interview have been somewhat unusual. During the last weeks I have become irritated at certain of the men I have interviewed who have seemed to claim too facilely that they have deep friendships. Somewhat perversely, with the idea of facing another of these rather facile types, I have conceived a set of impossible questions to test the depth of their male friendship.

1. If your friend called you at two in the morning and said, "I'm out here by the highway and I need you to come at once and help me bury a body, no questions asked," would you go?

2. If your friend needed to move in with you for a year, would you receive him?

3. If your friend asked you to mortgage your house for him, would you do it?

4. If your friend went crazy, difficult-crazy, would you keep him out of the hands of the mental health authorities by taking care of him yourself, for as long as it took?

I didn't expect people to answer yes. We moderns are far from being capable, most of us, of such lavish dispensing of our strained human resources. (Or else we have lost the habit of being truly engaged and unselfish.) I did expect to set my interviewees thinking to what extent their friendships were authentic.

As it happens, the first man I try my questions on is Richard Stone.

"I have a friend like that. The man I live with."

"You would actually take care of him if he went crazy? You know what an incredible strain that is?" I ask, disbelieving.

"Yes." The dry reply, its certainty vouched for by the silence surrounding it. No explanations, no hesitations, no fine print.

"You would bury the body?" I ask, still not believing.

"If he called me like that, yes."

"You would mortgage your house?"

"As it happens, I don't have a house. But I would do whatever he asked for financially."

Impressed, still somewhat doubting despite his obvious rectitude, I ask Stone to tell me about his friendship. To this point, on two continents, I had met no men who were so sworn to each other, despite the hundreds I had spoken with.

"I had just come to Antwerp and had an unhappy love affair. I was in my twenties, knew almost no one, and wanted to make friends. With tongue half in cheek, I advertised in the columns for a friend. Something like 'Young filmmaker seeks sincere friendship — free spirit with interesting character essential.'" Stone grins at the remembrance.

It annoys me unmercifully that the most serious male friendship I have so far encountered is between two homosexuals. It shames me and the other heterosexual men I have met. We need to do better. When it comes to friendship, *we* are unmanned.

8

Advocatus Diaboli:
Ferruccio, Count
of Chiaramonte

I continue my correspondence with American friends. I meet many
European men socially, but they seem very cautious. My personal
struggles have their victories, but they are small ones. Only a few
men I interview have real friends. The very best friends I have met
over several years are homosexual. It is not hopeful.

Then I encounter an extraordinary man who is, more than the
many other men I have met who have told me that friendship
between heterosexual men is dead, the *advocatus diaboli.* Ferruccio's
is the case for the end of true friendship between men.

• • •

"Since you wrote me and we first discussed the matter, I have
given some thought to the fact that I have no real friends. I am
now prepared to tell you why."

The man who speaks is Ferruccio, count of Chiaramonte, a
lean, elegant Florentine of very old family. He currently owns and
personally directs one of Italy's important business empires. Because of his historic family name, one is inclined to attribute the

man to his breeding. His calm detachment, the dark hair carefully cut and combed, the firm chin and the high-collared white tunic, the steady blue eyes, all bespeak an aristocratic self-discipline that at once flatters his hearer and intimidates.

Ferruccio is a man of great tradition and culture but also a graduate of an American business school. He has been described as "representing the fusion of European sophistication with American directness." He is an intellectual's author *and* a businessman, a man of celebrated *gentilezza* and an aggressive executive. As the interview, or rather his careful monologue, progresses, Ferruccio reveals a considerable complexity. He speaks slowly, measuring his thoughts into English words.

"Some kind of self-gratification, something you *need*, is at the basis of all kinds of love. What is friendship besides an audience?" He pauses for a moment to let me appreciate the realism, even the slight apparent cynicism, of these words.

"After looking at the way people relate, you will find that very seldom do you come across someone who really listens to you. To really listen, someone must love you in some way. Friendship is, first and foremost, an ear. And what you may give to be heard is often not very interesting stuff: just your noises, your silly puns, even your silent presence.

"If you have an important relationship with a woman in your life, you already have this plus all the satisfaction of romantic excitement and sexual satisfaction, don't you?"

It is a rhetorical question. He does not intend to press me to an answer. He merely expresses what he thinks for the benefit of my inquiry. In his characteristically detached manner, Ferruccio is only examining a difficult question, and as always with *calma e una certa distanza cerebrale*.

We sit quietly together in his large *salone,* itself the image of his personality: modern, pleasant, with excellent and functional white furniture and glass, impeccably arranged. Through the tall windows, across the Arno, one sees the sixteenth-century galleries of Vasari's Uffizi, the "offices" of the Medici, themselves once formidable businessmen and art patrons, like my host.

"Perhaps the tradition of male friendship was merely an artifact of Victorian, Anglo-Saxon culture. In a repressed time, a kind of love *manqué*.

"Let me try another approach." One senses that he is thinking aloud; the full flow of his argument is yet to be entered.

"There are different ways to create a hi-fi system. You can have components or you can have an integrated machine. The integrated machine takes less space, is less complex, more efficient."

I am a little shocked, amused, by his daring to be so contemporary, so apparently coarse in his metaphor. He knows he is teetering on the vulgar, and I am even a little excited to watch him so purposefully flout the European decorums that would eschew using any mechanical metaphors for relationships between people. Such deliberate hard-headedness is part of his approach to life, his learned, American, brutal facing of facts.

"Sometimes in life you don't find an integrated machine. Male friendship made a lot of sense when the attitudes toward women were different. In previous generations, a man would not even consider having a friendship with a woman, most especially with his own woman. But this has changed, as you know. And that affects male friendship with force; to take on male friendship, you need to take it away from a woman.

"In the nineteenth century, men couldn't exist without male friendship. They didn't have an integrated system in their affective life. Now, perhaps, male friendship is something one needs if you don't have the right kind of mate. Or, perhaps, if one doesn't have the ability to relate fully to women. But if one has an integrated system, you don't need components. Nowadays, it's hard to imagine how male friendship could exist."

This is also challenging, though I am not called upon to respond or argue with him. I *could* argue that I am friends, profoundly so, with my wife, and still I feel the need for men friends. I could say other things as well. Instead, I decide simply to listen. Perhaps Ferruccio is really justifying his own lack, or perhaps he is merely examining the issue with the greatest clarity he can achieve. I want to know where he will go from here.

"Let me take a more personal approach. When we spoke of this before, you dismissed too easily my idea that there was a problem of managing time. In truth, it affects one's possibilities. The more I go on in life, the more I have people who have a claim on me. And not just a professional claim; they want affectivity, affection. My mother is still alive. We have an active relationship. I see or telephone her every week. This seems to me the bare minimum, though many of my modern-minded friends, particularly in the States, think that at my age it is excessive. As I say, to me it seems absolutely minimal.

"And then I have brothers and sisters. Fortunately, I don't have intense relationships with all of them. But there is something. One sister is, indeed, my friend. She is truly kind, *gentile*. Kindness is rare. So she is very important to me. I usually see the other children once a week at dinner with my mother. Well, one dinner a week with my siblings, this is one seventh, since I work hard, of my capacity to relate to others, isn't it?"

Ferruccio seems to be arguing against me, but, again, this is a rhetorical question, thinking aloud, and not to be answered. I begin to be touched by the strong feelings he has revealed. The calm, rational man who speaks in the metaphors of hardware begins to take on another dimension. Could he not be the very image of the modern man, trying with great discipline to manage, with all his powers of rationality, the contrary and complex demands of his human nature?

"Then, I have children. The smaller ones can be treated in bulk. But the older ones demand tailored, individual contacts.

"Then I have my wife. We have agreed to separate. To me, she is very important. Of course, there are bruised feelings after all that has happened and a difficulty of finding common ground. But we work together; I see her every day. And if I don't give her attention for two days running, I wonder how she will feel.

"There is the woman I live with now. This is a new relationship, one that makes major claims on my time.

"I also have people who work for me. They don't all share their problems with me, but I am the local leader, and that implies some kind of human interaction.

"So what time is left?" Ferruccio pauses. A man used to being interviewed, he gives my pen time to catch up with my notetaking.

"I also feel friendship has to be done well. Some doctors give you the impression that you're the only patient. I respect that. I can't stand hollow relationships.

"So we move now from numbers to questions of intensity. Any kind of intensity is in conflict with any numbers at all. The average time spent by an executive on a decision is no more than ten minutes. One is constantly forced to make decisions without enough information, without enough thought. I find that horrible. But it is the same in my relationships. They all deserve more time; I want to give them more time.

"This horror I have of the superficial, the shallow, persuaded me, some eight years ago, simply to retire. To give up all the external claims and to lead a private life." He speaks of horror but his control is still there. He is always working at keeping a proper distance; it is part of his effort to do his best, part of the response to his horror. The only indication of a strain is a very slight swelling of the lips, the thin-pressed mouth allowed, just a little, to open.

"I moved to the beach, even wrote a book. I thought I could sustain autonomy. But then I became uneasy. This was my great failure in life. I couldn't change. I was programmed. I didn't have enough imagination to sustain an intense private life. I was programmed to be a leader. Out there by the ocean, I didn't have enough contacts to make life stimulating. I returned to start another business. It grew, mushroomed, and I am, once again, overwhelmed.

"It didn't happen at first. Not for years. The job is decision-making, but as the business grows, my decisions, though bigger, become increasingly based on inadequate information and study. As for people, I had thought I would beat the game by surrounding myself with people who would be intensely involved with me, friends, really. It was the integrated hi-fi principle. I even brought my wife into the work. But it has not happened as I had optimistically hoped. Yes, we are all in the same building, but increasingly all we do is discuss and try to solve business problems. That's all, and we do it superficially."

Another man would allow himself to show weariness at such a recital of failure and disappointment. Not this one. I think that his determined poise despite, perhaps because of, the mechanical metaphors so purposefully used, is nearly gallant.

"Then comes the annual budget. You make yourself look forward to the coming year. And you find that ninety-five percent of what you will have is already committed by previous history, previous decisions. Only five percent remains. That time constitutes all your discretionary hours. Well, you can only invest it in one person. For me that person is the woman I live with.

"Even here," he pauses briefly, "we have to be very patient, middle-aged, I would say, *molto saggio,* very wise. So where is the time for friendship?"

I sense he is arguing with my unrealistic idealism, but again, no answer is expected.

"I want to pick up something I said at the beginning. I think that at bottom I would not want to be a friend to a man who has male friends. At bottom, I suspect, intense male friendship is somehow, somewhere, antiwoman.

"I was on a talk show defending a book I had written and another writer there said, 'I hate to be in a place where there's only men — barracks, locker rooms.' I am like that. In all previous generations, the bond between men was based, in part, on envy and contempt of women. Racism of a sort. I have always felt that. I was in a Jesuit school as a boy. It was filled with antifeminine Roman Catholic tradition, an antiwoman atmosphere. I felt isolated from the other boys, not being one of the top athletes. It was something instinctive, too. To be very honest, I felt that women *listened* to me better.

"Nowadays, there are perhaps only two kinds of situations where intense male relationships would make a lot of sense and be very attractive experiences. One is war. War, or other types of great physical danger, stops all this flow of ordinary events I have been discussing. At such times, there can be very intense exchanges between people. In France, there is even a phrase for the nostalgia: *une très belle guerre,* a very beautiful war.

"War, of course, is always terrible. It is also full of peaks, of deep human contact, of life lived with great intensity. Yet this only makes it, paradoxically, a tragedy for survivors. Some of my own relatives have been left truly high and dry by their inability to recreate in daily life what they had in war. You see, despite the intense exchange between people, when the war ends, you don't necessarily keep your friends.

"The other circumstance where male friendship makes sense is in intellectual life. If you are a genuine intellectual and have extreme and specialized cultural interests, there are only so many people with whom to share them. You can find great pleasure in sharing that little niche, that inner wealth. It's rarer and rarer to discover such individuals. On the other hand, if you find a woman with the same interests who is reasonably attractive, it's hard to imagine you wouldn't end up in bed together, isn't it?

"Before you came, I looked up some words, because it is hard for me to express all this in English. There is one that has no adequate translation but that I think is central to friendship. It is the idea of a genuine and deep attentiveness, a positive regard. Perhaps, you could say quite simply, kindness.

"It is harder and harder to find kindness in the world." Ferruccio did not pause to make any sentimental emphasis.

"Modern society is often accused. Perhaps the lack of kindness is, indeed, due to the modern shortening of the time span you can give to anything, to the flood of communication within which we live and drown, to the greater number of problems treated every day. You need to be ever more productive, you have to go to the essentials very fast, so you can't treat the surroundings, which may turn out to be the most meaningful.

"Certainly this pace of modern life makes depth, in anything, difficult to achieve. But what seems to me the increasing lack of kindness in people may simply be an artifact of *my* growing older. It may always have been this way. We blame society for what may only be the result of our collective amnesia. Because we remember so little, every generation discovers basic human attitudes anew.

"One that I discover is the inability of most people to be interested in other people. It's so rare when you find people who listen, then think about what you are saying, and then answer. It can create very strong links between individuals. It happened with you, Stuart, when we met, only briefly, ten years ago. I knew we were going to meet and had read one of your books purposely for that reason. I had thought about it. And then I discussed my thoughts with you. We spoke for two hours. I remember that you were well impressed. Surprised, at first, and then pleased in a fairly significant way. I am like that. When I meet people, I think about them before we are to see each other. I engage with their interests, who they are. I have often been told it moves them. But as I get older I find that not many other people do the same. That is what I mean by kindness.

"Apparently, the basic human atttitude is one of indifference. I am overwhelmed by this fact. We are all brought up in a Christian culture or, more simply, a bourgeois culture. We are taught that we must care for people: parents, children, spouse, whoever comes near us. Some individuals take it seriously. I probably did, though

I could laugh at it, too. I thought the relationship between parents and children, between lovers, perhaps friends, would transcend basic human limits.

"But I've seen, as one grows older, that people care less and less. Even your own parents."

Ferruccio stops to think, then to make himself absolutely clear says, "Please don't misunderstand me. My parents were very good to me. And I think I have been good to them. I don't need to go on the couch to work through disasters and problems with my parents. It's just that, quite simply, I've seen them rigidify, the same as their arteries, and occurring at the same period and for the same reason. As we approach the passage toward death, people go back to a fetal position. A stiff crouch. As if to prepare for a jump. Older people no longer have the ability to radiate. They need all the energy for themselves.

"The elimination of interest in others is something that happens fast. Not only in old age; it begins in middle age. The romantic poets are full of this idea. But then, I do not like romantic poetry. Just as I am more and more suspicious of romantic love.

"Will you have some tea?"

A servant in a white jacket has appeared in response to the touch of a button. Chiaramonte himself pours the tea into old white china cups, but he only tastes his and then puts it down. The refreshment is for the guest.

"I'm privileged in many respects," he continues. I nod; it is manifestly true.

"Others have more excuse for whatever villainy they have done to me. But it is always unpleasant. Even though I have never really been subjected to rejection, betrayal. It's just a basic coldness that people have.

"It is the same with young people. As I said, I have teenagers and younger children both. I appreciate ever more the openness of the younger ones. The adolescents, however, are so truly selfish that it is fascinating. My own sons. They are just not interested. I know how to create a good relationship with them but the moment I say, 'How about me?' I receive indifference.

"I suppose I am not very optimistic about human nature in general. This pessimism, this souring, has happened to me in a rich society during peaceful times, to a person who is privileged in many ways, including my personal life! As one grows older, one becomes more fine-tuned to people's attitudes. You see that it is not Shakespeare with which we are surrounded. It is Ingmar Bergman. The results are very disappointing."

Ferruccio looks out the window at the muddy river, then turns back. "Of course, I myself am no better this way.

"A few years ago, I thought of myself as better than others, kinder. Now I'm only aware of being better in a very small way, and locally, with people close to me. I am better because I have help, and that saves time, and also because I am very conscious of time's shortness, so I use it with great thoughtfulness. I realize that others have more handicaps than I do and I have become more patient with them. I have always felt a sense of duty, obligation, about my privileges.

"But, as I say, in how little am I really superior? What does it really mean? About a dozen people, at the most thirty, have my attention. But I am as indifferent as everyone else to people outside the circle.

"My capacity for not joining Amnesty International is enormous." Ever poised, Ferruccio pauses for rueful emphasis.

I asked him if the recent separation from his wife has not disillusioned him, made him particularly sensitive to this "indifference."

"Nothing teaches you more than a separation from someone you love. My wife was at the center; now she moves aside. *And you find you can adjust.* One of the ways you adjust is to forget.

"Of course, not the essential, not the need to continue some kind of relationship. The fact that it seems even easier for her than me to forget has nothing to do with it. Perhaps that's my defense.

But it is interesting. You just dismiss the details; you don't have time and so much the better."

"What kind of details?" I am pressing Ferruccio. He hesitates, then decides to be frank.

"Details that make the texture of the day. Whatever details that make for conversation at the end of it. In our case, to allude only to rather recent events, it is details such as discussing Maria's new relationship. Despite everything, I was not jealous. I am not a jealous person. I was interested and I cared. You feel with a subject you come back to, day after day, that it is meaningful, and rare.

"But now my wife would not discuss such matters with me. I am not her friend anymore."

This time there is a long silence.

"The last thing we did together was to visit the museum. We had a common emotion looking at the face of a very tiny Greek statue. The head of a girl. It was so touching, almost transparent. We felt that common inner movement, which was like when we were young and first together.

"It was on the way back to Florence, from Athens, that we decided to separate. But we resolved to continue sharing all. Except we don't anymore.

"This cutting off is simply necessary to live through the day. Otherwise, one would be too torn. So if you're like that, how can you expect others to be different? You don't want solitude. So you're back to the beginning.

"Few people analyze such events and draw conclusions. Perhaps it's best for them. But if you're conscious, you can't really return to innocence. All at once the person is not really there anymore. You find it is normal not to be concerned anymore. At the same time, you regret it's happening. The process of getting someone out of your blood is a difficult but very interesting experience. The horrible aspect is, you learn it is possible. This you will never forget."

A silence. In a moment I catch the significance. This man who takes time so seriously has used up the time he has to spend with me. It had been clear at the outset, though unstated, that we could not talk indefinitely. I regret it because the talk has been very good, because, aloof though he is in his way, this would be a most "interesting" man (as he put it) to be friends with. I am so grateful for the effort he has made to articulate himself on friendship, so difficult a subject for most men, that I am satisfied to leave without any murmur.

But it is Ferruccio who continues talking. We move past the mirrored antique doors of the salon into the spacious hall, bright with electric candelabra and the reflections of more mirrors on the walls. Even as I have my hand on the brass handle of the old front door, rushing in a calm way so as to express my gratitude by politely disappearing, he talks. It is a little different from what he has been saying, I think. Just a little change in his tone.

"It's terrible you know. I just received a long letter from a man. We were in the army together. It was a very detailed and warm letter. He's going to come and visit me, although we haven't seen each other in eighteen years. I dread it. I know he will be disappointed. I, too, will be disappointed. There is nothing between us but memories. You see, I haven't time to include him in my life. And we are very different. His life experience has been provincial and quiet; mine, almost too international and full."

Ferruccio is not a man to ask for help, though I sense he wants me to help him with this. But it is time for me to go. The afternoon has already turned to early evening. Time for his next appointment. His life was hurrying him forward, a very sincere man. He needs, with great courtesy, to get on with it; to get rid of me, along with the thought of the imminent arrival of his old friend. For now.

"Let's talk again, in a few months, if you have questions." His last words.

Despite everything Ferruccio has so well denied about the possibilities for friendship, it crosses my mind, as I turn the beautiful old door handle, that he still shares my own hopes. Indeed, I am surprised, as I leave, that despite his crushing summary — so clear and elegant and forceful — of all that stands in the way of true friendship between men, I feel not depressed but purged. As if his moving statement is the emotional catharsis of the real obstacles. Now I at least, and perhaps later he, having paid our conscious dues to the terrible difficulties that stand between men, could with renewed energy take up the quest.

I suppose if I had said so before I left him, he would have thought me, though too polite to remark it, a "romantic."

9

Male Friendship in Europe: Continuity, Obligation, and Complicity

Ferruccio Chiaramonte is not a typical Italian. His origins, his intellect, his discipline, his wealth, and his aloofness all make him exceptional. But I found in interviewing many other Italian men that they too were most often friendless. Much of Italy has become as modern in outlook, laws, habits, and customs as the rest of the Western world. While Italian good humor, warmth, and conviviality have survived despite the rapid social changes, friendship is more an institution remembered than one actually lived.

This discovery was among a series of disappointments. I had gone to Europe with the thought that the death of friendship between men in America must be due to our country's peculiar history, that in other modern, equally urban and developed societies there would be more solid traditions of human relationship and I would find many living examples of what I was seeking. That in going there I could discover and then bring back ways of being, insights, arts of friendship, if you will, that could serve my own needs and those of others. Indeed, most Americans, even university experts on friendship — one professor from Michigan especially comes to mind — have the same idealized notion of Europe.

So do some Europeans. At first they would exclaim to me, "Friendship? Really? How American to write a book on such a subject! In your society all these personal matters are 'problems,' aren't they? One doesn't worry about such matters here. I suppose we take friendship for granted." But as I dug deeper, another picture emerged. A Belgian attorney confessed that it wasn't "so different here." True, he had taken the same commuter train every day for the last eleven years, played cards and chatted with the same men, discussed politics. But, he continued, "I wouldn't say that any one of all these men I know — including others on a weekend soccer team — is really friends. Not in that deep and involved sense you mean. Now my *wife* has friends. They talk for hours, they fight and make up. It's amazing how close they are." His voice trailed off, filled with wonder and envy.

Gradually, after a number of such encounters, I confronted European men in a new way, telling them that the great tradition of close male friendship seemed dead in America and, to my surprise, in Europe too. Astonishingly, when I put it that way, they agreed. But some continued to protest that I would still find it if I kept looking, but elsewhere. In England, or in France, or in Germany, for example.

But my English interviews turned up the same disappointing results. Indeed, the famous men's clubs in England — one of our classic images for a social situation where close friendship may arise and be sustained — are closing for lack of members. As early as 1960, C. S. Lewis observed the decline of English friendship. Though ensconced as professor in the male society of Cambridge, he had nevertheless lamented:

> To the Ancients, Friendship seemed the happiest and most fully human of all loves . . . The modern world ignores it. We admit of course that besides a wife and family a man needs a few "friends." But the very tone of admission, and the sort of

acquaintanceships which those who make it would describe as "friendships," show clearly that what they are talking about has very little to do with that *Philia* which Aristotle classified among the virtues or that *Amicitia* on which Cicero wrote a book. It is something quite marginal; not a main course in life's banquet; a diversion; something that fills up the chinks of one's time.

In France, it was the same. Though some foreigners had pointed out to me that France did have a twentieth-century fictional oeuvre about friendship — Saint-Exupéry, Antoine Blondin, Rogier Nimier, Michel Déon — and though they insisted there must be a reality to match it, when I went to France myself, my interviews uncovered an emptiness. Even scaling the heights of the French intellectual elite, I learned that one sociological authority after another ruefully agreed with my finding that French male friendship was largely dead. They would present their personal histories as typical: their friends in adult life were "women — women listened" to them "better"; over the years their male friends had been lost through "the attrition of family, work, and time." Often brilliantly they analyzed certain of the causes: "The feminization of society . . . the modern woman occupies a great place . . . the diaspora of modern times . . . geographic factors . . . the *enfermement,* the enclosing, of professional life. Before, people imitated one another to learn a craft. But once you have a bureaucratic civilization, à la Kafka, a professional racecourse with rules of selective promotion, you begin to get *obsession*; your whole life, including your social life, becomes *strategy.* With this, the hierarchy and conformity of modern life constantly forces you away from people, makes you choose sides." A journalist, Christiane Collange, who has just completed an extensive study of men all over France, eighty percent of them in small provincial cities, sadly confirms the Parisian experts: "Only one in ten French men has close friends — tops!"

And in Germany, too, the same response. One social

philosopher, though admitting like many other men I talked to throughout Europe that he "hadn't really thought about the subject before," was even moved to say during our interview that perhaps in Germany and elsewhere we have a "crisis of friendship."

Did all this make me conclude that European relationships between men are exactly the same as those in the United States? I think it would be wrong to go that far. What is the same is the general lack of active, deeply felt, constantly present (either in one's sentiments or one's day-to-day physical existence) male friendships. To find a pair of modern European men who deeply love one another, carry one another in their hearts, are daily in one another's actual lives in some way, is as rare as for American men. Like their American counterparts, many European men will casually claim to have friends. What they mean is that they have relationships of affectionate understanding with one or more men, usually people they remember from school days. Or they may be men with whom they once worked, or work now, or whom they met on vacation.

Nevertheless, these ordinary, warm relationships between men that do exist are positively different in certain ways from most of their American counterparts. When a European enters into any personal relationship, including affectionate friendliness, there is still an inner expectation that it will continue, that it will not change nor be given up. Hence, even when a European man doesn't see the other for years, or even think of him except in the most glancing way during all that time, when the two chance to meet, or when one calls, there is no real surprise. In some dim and unspoken way, there was always a latent but active expectation of continuity.

In the United States, on the other hand, by the time one has served several years of adulthood, the friends already lost are viewed as lost; there is not the same expectation that a relationship will continue. There may have been the wish that it endure; there will very likely be some kind of secret disappointment and bitterness that it did not; but there is no inner voice that simply says, "This relationship, like every other, still exists the way old stone walls still exist back in the home village: that is the way life is." A product of what was, until very recently, a much more stable society, the contemporary urban European still feels that life is not so radically changeable.

With this often unconscious expectation of a certain constancy comes a feeling of obligation. It is hard to say which is derived from the other or if they simply appear together in the imprint that his culture still gives to the European's psyche. There exists a whole network of pressures to behave reliably. A European grows up in a certain social milieu. That group has its rules, its demands, that it makes on all its members for mutual favors, for taking time to be available to the needs of one another. One never outgrows, even today, the sense that one's very existence depends on meeting the demands of others. This amounts to, at a minimum, a kind of polite conformity that does not admit the most radical American individualism. As a European, you may not want to do a favor for the childhood friend who calls after many years, but you do what is expected, anyway. Otherwise, so you have been taught to feel, everything will fall apart.

In America, at least for a very substantial proportion of our liberated population, such a notion of social obligation is almost entirely gone. The inner taboo on total individualism has nearly died. In Europe, that older pattern persists in the personal mental structure. As a European, one knows that self-expression is not everything, that one must rouse oneself to respond, to invite, to take some care.

The idea of complicity between two particular individuals, which also gives a different coloration to European friendships, is related to obligation partly by opposition. Complicity is in part a reaction to the idea of a generalized social obligation. Yet, in actual practice, the two can also work together.

A tough engineer, Portuguese, something of a buccaneer of

international commerce, told me: "Yes, indeed, real friendship is rare. Friendship is *complicité*, but even my wife has no true *complicité* with me. For example, she will be very loyal, understanding, and loving, but she is not about to help me have a love affair. So, you see, even in the closest of modern relationships, marriage, there is no real *complicité*."

This was, on a couple of counts, a most astonishing set of statements. First, the repeated use of the word *complicity*. I couldn't imagine an American using that word as a synonym for friendship; that is, if I understood what the word meant in French. Second, the idea that a wife should be a friend to the extent of aiding and abetting the husband's love affairs, while it had a certain dreamy appeal, seemed too unrealistic even for my own high expectations of friendship.

Though *complicité* rang in my ears, I dismissed it and his excessively idealistic notion of friendship as eccentric to this particular Iberian wheeler-dealer.

But the word kept coming up. A Belgian expert on international development who lives in Africa much of the time begins his remarks by saying, "Friendship is *une complicité*: a secret understanding." A Swiss homosexual painter says, "In the case of the man I feel closest to — not my lover — friendship is a certain *complicité*; we share a rather acid view of things." A Polish refugee physicist, heterosexual, now living in France, remarks with equal spontaneity, "The man I most like shares with me *une complicité* which creates a gratifying separation from others."

The derivation is *cum-plex* (*cum*, with; *plex*, folded): that which is folded with, united. This certainly suggests a vivid intimacy. If, as I imagined, however, the word is like the English *complicity*, there is more to it. Indeed, the primary meaning was the same, according to the *Larousse*: *complicité* from *complice*, in modern French, meaning, "he who participates in a crime, a wrong . . . a fault of another." I learn from looking up *complice*, as if it were an English word, in the *Oxford English Dictionary*:

"Adoption of French *complice* . . . specifically an associate in crime
. . . now ACCOMPLICE."

This was an extraordinary cluster of concepts with which to
define such friendships as exist between European men: two
people united in crime, two accomplices in a wrong. *Larousse* went
on to detail a secondary meaning: "By extension, one uses the
word *complice* even when there is no notion of culpability, but
simply of mystery, secrecy."

"Separation" from others, "mystery," "secret understanding,"
and "participation in a crime" are four ideas that flow rather easily
into one another. The package that is the French *complicité* seems to
contain them all. These Europeans, a mixed group of French
speakers from Portugal, Belgium, Switzerland, Poland, and
France, all associate friendship with a word that has the idea of
crime at its core. For them, friendship is, at the least, a secret understanding; mutual access to a mystery about which others are allowed to know nothing, a separation from the norms and expectations of society. In short, I realized, it includes the idea of revolt.

It is in this sense that the widespread notion of complicity in
friendship is the reciprocal, the paradoxical opposite, of the equally
important European notion of obligation. If European personal
relationships still have a different flavor from American ones, it is
in part because such intimacy as exists can be defined as a relatively
sharp secession from the obligations of society, from the norms of
whatever official world. But these secret intimate relationships, in
turn, are permeated with and supported by the general collective
sense of obligation. Thus, in friendship one is obliged to keep the
secret understanding, to maintain the particular mystery, as one
has other obligations in all European social relationships, even the
most superficial ones. Implicitly, if necessary, if some ultimate
need arises, one is socially obligated to express the revolt of friendship in antisocial crime.

I came to believe that complicity is a notion that can help
illuminate our contemporary American lack of male friendship.

True friendship has, among other qualities, that of a secession from the socially conventional. It is the locus of our daring to be thick as thieves. It is the private society where we can be truly unofficial, happily or unhappily crazy together. Where the social world demands conformity, here we can be free. It is the place for true anarchy, no government. The notion of friendship as allowing and even fostering a profound inner freedom is one we need to bring back to our sense of what serious adult relationships can be.

10

The Fear
of Homosexuality

Both in America and Europe I encountered the notion that the fear of being taken for a homosexual or, worse, becoming one is a main factor keeping adult men from close friendships. In the United States, in Germany, in Belgium, France, England and Switzerland, in Portugal, Spain, and Italy, literally everyone I talked to mentioned it. The universality of this view was astonishing.

While the fear is indeed rampant in our society, and while it exercises a restraining effect on certain of the more tender possibilities for adult male friendship, it is not the decisive factor in inhibiting friendship per se. Many economic and social factors are much more important.

Indeed, not a single man among the hundreds I interviewed, even when I have pressed with what I thought to be considerable force and artfulness, has explained just how the fear of homosexuality keeps him from having close friends.

The fact that there has never been in my experience any evidence that the fear of homosexuality is very important in preventing friendship will be treated by some as evidence in itself that it is important. It is this sort of perverse (if the word may be allowed) logic that C. S. Lewis so adroitly lampoons in discussing a closely related matter: the contemporary tendency to reduce such few male friendships as do survive to the homosexual:

> It has actually become necessary in our time to rebut the theory that every firm and serious friendship is really homosexual. The dangerous word *really* is important. To say that every Friendship is consciously and explicity homosexual would be too obviously false; the wiseacres take refuge in the less palpable charge that it is really — unconsciously, cryptically, in some Pickwickian sense — homosexual. And this, though it cannot be proved, can never of course be refuted. The fact that no positive evidence of homosexuality can be discovered in the behaviour of two friends does not disconcert the wiseacres at all: "That," they say gravely, "is just what we should expect." The very lack of evidence is thus treated as evidence.

Similar confusion obtains, in a more general way, with nearly everything concerning the topic of homosexuality. Talk about it and your motives are suspect. Don't talk about it and your motives are suspect.

Nothing in recent history makes the situation easier. The rise of gay liberation movements, for example, has not clarified our thinking about homosexuality in general nor its incidence in the population nor its naturalness in human beings. Gays themselves differ as to whether they think of homosexuality as latent within every man or woman or a sexual preference of the few not really elected but produced by childhood events, perhaps even genetic in origin. The psychiatric establishment, to whom we would have turned for some scientific clarity about all this, has with embarrassment abandoned the field for the moment. It once thought homosexuality was a disease; now it is equally certain it is not.

Try to think about homosexuality in itself and you don't know what to think. One must fall back on whatever common sense can be mustered.

Let us state the obvious: physical affection among men is not a sign of homosexuality. This will reassure the male reader who hesitates to reach out, literally, toward a man friend. Again, C. S. Lewis makes the point:

> Kisses, tears and embraces [between men] are not in themselves evidence of homosexuality. The implications would be, if nothing else, too comic. Hrothgar embracing Beowulf, Johnson embracing Boswell (a pretty flagrantly heterosexual couple) and all those hairy old toughs of centurions in Tacitus, clinging to one another and begging for last kisses when the legion was broken . . . all pansies? If you can believe that you can believe anything.

As subjects of routine and general preoccupation, the fear of homosexuality and its purportedly dulling effect on friendship are rather new in Western history. Until recently, even in the northern cultures, men could express tender closeness without the bizarre fear of being thought lovers. Lord Nelson was a man of such daring physical courage that he was a legendary hero in his own lifetime. Toward the end of the Battle of Trafalgar — in which his daring probably saved England from French invasion — after having exposed himself for hours to enemy sniper fire in order to inspire his own men to their victory, he is shot down. "They have done for me at last," he says. "Yes, my backbone is shot through." His friend Hardy, the commander of his flagship, receives the dying Nelson's last words. They are for his mistress and his friend: "You know what to do. And take care of my dear Lady Hamilton, Hardy. Take care of poor Lady Hamilton. Kiss me, Hardy." And it is recorded that Captain Hardy

> now knelt down and kissed his cheek, when his Lordship said: "Now I am satisfied; thank God, I have done my duty." Captain Hardy stood for a minute or two in silent contemplation: he then knelt down again, and kissed his Lordship's forehead. His Lordship said: "Who is that?" The Captain answered: "It

is Hardy," to which his Lordship replied, "God bless you, Hardy!"

The point is not that masculinity and homosexuality are incompatible. Some particularly tough types — Billy the Kid, Wyatt Earp, and Lord Kitchener, for example — have been homosexuals. Rather, the point is that until Nelson's time, at least, warm, physical, friendly behavior between men did not call up automatic images of a minority sexual preference.

My impression from interviewing older men and women is that this widespread fear of homosexuality is no more than fifty or sixty years old. Literary sources confirm this impression.

By 1960, C. S. Lewis has to complain about the necessity of "demolishing" the confusion of homosexuality and friendship. A mere thirty-three years before, another English man of letters, Edward Garnett, is able to write as if such a confusion could never occur to any reasonable person. In 1927, Garnett published his collection of letters from the great novelist Joseph Conrad. The letters record the growth and progress of a friendship between the two literary men.

Garnett was, at the outset, a publisher's reader in London; Conrad a tough adventurer and a sailor. When Conrad began to write fiction in midlife, Garnett rendered him the precious service of recommending that a publisher buy his first novel, *Almayer's Folly*. Over some years of great critical success but financial failure, Garnett persistently encouraged the sailor to become the master of fiction he, with time, became. The friendship lasted thirty years. Both men got married, had children, and faced the trials of middle and old age — the sickness of spouses, concerns about offspring, financial problems, and struggles with the creative life, even with celebrity. Here is Garnett's description of what would prove to be their last meeting. At his country house, the writer, aged now, has been suffering from illness for many years:

> Conrad had been fatigued, I think in the week, by visitors, transatlantic and others, pressing in with their homage, and

after our last hour's talk together something moved me as we said good-night, to put his hand to my lips. He then embraced me with a long and silent pressure. The next morning as we stood talking in his study, when the car was announced, he suddenly snatched from a shelf overhead a copy of the Polish translation of *Almayer's Folly*, wrote an inscription in it and pressed it into my hands. When I looked I saw that the date he had written in it was the date of our first meeting, thirty years before.

That quality of intimate feeling between two male friends is almost unthinkable nowadays. Probably few men would even allow themselves such feelings, much less dream of expressing them.

Instead, all men secretly know how often they shrink away from one another. Often, a whole set of programmed reactions is put into motion. They can arise, for example, from an innocent approach at a bar. In *Something Happened*, Joseph Heller captures this version of the reflexive withdrawal:

> I've never learned how to make friends in strange cities. Men who strike up conversations wth me appear homosexual and drive me off.
> "I've got to go now. I have this friend I have to meet."
> "Take care."
> All I know how to do in a strange city is read the local newspapers.

Or the programmed reactions can arise from a glance into the eyes of a stranger at a party, a sense that someone is looking, really looking, at you. From a man you know becoming suddenly very warm to you. From the quietness of teatime when a new man is introduced and you find him handsome, brilliant, soft, or strong.

Once, during the early weeks in Belgium, I made an effort to catch my particular version of the inner process of fear of homosexuality. Jacqueline and I had been having tea in a large house in Ghent; the fall leaves had just started to turn. The doorbell rang, and after a few moments our host introduced a man holding the hands of two silent little children.

The new man is tall, slender, quiet. Around thirty-five, I should say. He is obviously refined. There is something quite gentle about him, something relaxing, sensitive. I notice he is handsome in a Nordic sort of way. I do not feel especially drawn to him but I have a positive feeling about him.

And then, despite the normality of the teatime moment, the clarity of my own lack of any strong interest in this stranger, the fact that I am with my wife and he with who I take to be his children, I observe it start, seemingly of its own accord — the inner dialogue about possible homosexuality. The reflexive series of silent half questions come very fast — the way thought can, when it is programmed. It is so swift and fragmentary, so complex, so full of contrary notes and hesitations and fears, that it is hard to catch, much less record:

"Is he?

"Does he think I am?

"Why would he think I am, if, indeed, he thinks I am?

"Why do I wonder about whether he is?

"I must doubt myself. Is there something wrong with me?

"This is nonsense, Stuart!

"Yes, I know, but then why am I doing it? And what is *he* thinking?

"Maybe it's coming from him?

"This is ridiculous."

Were it not so sticky a matter, from a certain point of view it would be amusing to watch ourselves going through such contortions. What are the historical causes of this new sort of inner self-torture? Above all, the frequently simplistic popularization of Freud's work has encouraged people to interpret all human encounters in sexual terms. One is encouraged to believe that in the realm of the interpersonal, sex is the sole fundamental reality. When we feel even the most casual attraction to another human being, we assume that it must, *really,* be sexual. If it is not, then we must be hiding something from ourselves.

The progress of such ideas began with the Victorians. For reasons having to do with the sort of discipline necessary to building and holding a commercial empire, they repressed and denied sexuality to a degree and with a universality unknown in any earlier time. Naturally, everyone became obsessed with what was forbidden. Freud exposed and exploded the repression and the obsession. Afterward, however, society continued the reaction and overemphasized the importance of sex as a human motivator. In some pseudosophisticated way, we are still repetitively living out a blind rebellion against the Victorians — with a vengeance that frequently traps us.

As part of the same historical process, the progressive liberation of women has combined, in several ways, with the idea of all relationships being sexual to create the hovering fear of homosexuality that clouds the minds and feelings of contemporary men.

First, if all relationships are sexual and women are sexually available to men as never before, then a heterosexual man has no excuse for spending time in any significant relationship that isn't overtly heterosexual.

Second, once women are liberated and more and more "equal" to men — doing the same jobs, participating in the same sports, even joining armies — then the definition of *manliness* becomes more and more problematic for each and every man. Men are exhorted from childhood days: "Be a man!" But because it is not so clear, nowadays, what that means, men must really *work* at retaining some sense of gender identity. Most men, wrongly of course, confuse sexual preference with their gender identity, homosexuality with effeminacy, heterosexuality with masculinity. Therefore, part of the work every heterosexual man must perform to "be a man" is never, ever, to make the slightest move that would cause himself or others to think his sexual preference in doubt.

Third, the liberation of women, as Ferruccio Chiaramonte implies in his repudiation of the possibilities for male friendship, has also brought the possibilities for sex and friendship together. In general, men and women can now have fuller relationships than at any previous time. Because — the pseudo-Freudian truth again — all relationships are fundamentally sexual and because you can have your sex and your friendship over there, well, what the hell are you doing with your male friend over here?

· · ·

In fact and in practice, there seems to be a separation between male friendship and homosexuality. The most striking examples are among homosexuals themselves. Numerous homosexual men — ranging in age from twenty-five to fifty and in style from swish to macho — have informed me that friendship is, indeed, absolutely critical to their lives. Then they have added, "I have never slept with him," or, like Richard Stone, "We tried but it didn't work," or "We did it once but it wasn't particularly interesting."

The same homosexual men are absolutely excoriating about straight men's fear of homosexuality. They particularly delight in lampooning the fear of touching another man, stage whisper, "lest it lead to seduction!" It is not, they claim, that it might *not* lead to seduction; it's that it usually doesn't.

As one English homosexual put it to me, "I am frequently surprised by this myself. I have occasion, in my business, to travel all over the world. I was astonished and delighted, of course, to see Arab men casually walking down the street arm in arm, or even holding hands. But it was only when I actually lived in the Middle East that I learned that these same men are very rarely lovers or really homosexual. They might, on occasion, because women were unavailable, sleep with the visiting northern tourist. But it was almost unheard of for them to sleep with their beloved friends.

"Once I lived in Hong Kong. It was during the Vietnam War, and there were many thousands of South Vietnamese boys and young men who had been sent there to avoid the draft. Well, I fell in with a group of these young men in their twenties. First I made friends with one, then I became part of his extended group of comrades. One evening I got a call. 'Will you come over? I'm alone tonight and my wife is away and I don't want to sleep alone.'

"So I caught a cab and went over. And all we did was, literally, sleep together!

"You see, male friendship is very important in that part of the world, particularly when the men are young. Moreover, they are not afraid of touch or intimate contact. But they simply detest sleeping alone. It makes them uneasy."

"Did you touch when you were in bed?" I asked casually, trying to pretend the same nonchalance as he exhibited about male physical intimacy.

"Well, I suppose in the course of the night my leg fell upon his or something like that. Can't remember, to tell you the truth. I can add that any number of American soldiers were scandalized by seeing Vietnamese GIs in full battle dress walking up the road holding hands. They didn't know what to make of it. I heard from American officers, older men, that they had to get used to the same sort of thing with the ROK troops during Korea."

Another striking interview I had, also with an Englishman, further emphasized the separation between friendship and homosexuality, this time between heterosexual men who as boys had experimented with homosexuality in ways typical of their social milieu. This forty-year-old man now works in Berlin for an international consortium of glass manufacturers. Though married, he evinces a rather typical interest in chasing women, and he actually does so, with considerable success, during his far-flung business trips.

"Yes, I had an extremely close friend. David meant the world to me. Our friendship was formed around the challenges of growing up. We saw each other constantly between the ages of ten and twenty-three. He taught me so much.

"I yearn for him even though I don't know where he is now. Although our lives have taken us far apart, as the Spaniards say, he is *la media naranja,* the other half of the orange.

"You know of course that in England boys of a certain social class, between the ages of fourteen and sixteen, are often homosexual partners. At boarding school their education is sexually segregated, you see, and the libido is rising. You make do with boys. Jerk each other off, that sort of thing. But, curiously, I never did it with David. He was a brother."

I am impressed and depressed at the idea that people have that it is the fear of homosexuality which keeps men apart. I know, from my years of leading encounter groups at Esalen, that most men have just a little doubt about their sexuality and secretly suspect they might, just perhaps, "really be queer." I have seen the most brawny types, over and over, confess to that in encounter groups. And other types as well.

I also know some men who have confronted that doubt and found it foolish, sometimes by actually experimenting as adults with a homosexual experience to see what would happen. This second group of men has no more friends than the first group.

Six Months Before the Meeting with Wreston in Spain

The homosexual business came up today. This morning, passing through Seattle on a consultant job, I dropped in on Wreston at his art school. I wanted his advice about a problem I was having in writing a short story.

As usual, he took my request with total seriousness.

"You have got to work at it, to chisel away at it, if you see what I mean. But to keep the whole in view, even if you can't see it yet. You have got to stop, when you can't go on, and do something else. Sharpen your pencils, fiddle around."

Not spectacular advice, nothing profoundly original about it — commonplace shop talk, really, But it is what I need to hear at this moment, working on this particular problem. It helps.

As I listen, I begin to experience a generalized pleasure, due I suppose to his caring about me, his passionate engagement — for my sake — with his little suggestions. But so many people I have interviewed lately have told me that fear of homosexuality is what keeps men apart that I find myself suddenly wondering if my rosy good feeling doesn't have some erotic flavor to it. Something vague, general, *perhaps* sexual in some way. Drawing me toward Wreston as he talks.

I do not move. I sit in my chair. Alarmed but controlled, I maintain my face as it looked before, smiling with the pleasure of getting useful advice.

What the hell am I supposed to do?

Fuck him? Do I want to fuck him? What in the world would it be like to fuck a man???

No. That's not it. But I need to give the impulse, whatever it may be, some imaginative release at least.

My mind creates an image for me. But it is almost as alarming as the first generalized impulse whose force I had wanted to attenuate by giving it an imaginative expression.

I see myself, in my imagination, rising from the old wooden chair on which I sit and making the first few steps toward him. Then, caressing, with my outstretched hand, his old head. Smoothing his wrinkled gray hair. This old Celtic-Mongol. Ruddy of skin, with slits for eyes, creased and beaten and passionate and brilliant.

I don't do it, of course. Men don't do that anymore. Besides, where might it lead? Might it lead to the bed?

I doubt it.

So what is one to do with this tender energy?

The Next Day

Yes. There was *something* sexual in what happened, or in what didn't happen. Better, something "erotic." A little broader.

But even to say that is not truly accurate.

Intimacy is a complex experience. Love is a complex experience. As Wilhelm Reich tells us, love is energy, energy that one experiences in one's body.

My problem with Wreston is not that I am afraid I will go to bed with him and that, then, I will have spoiled our budding friendship, at the least. Or perhaps proved myself "queer."

No, I am not going to go to bed with him. I have been brainwashed by the "sexualists." My true problem, rather, is what to do with my *tenderness* toward him. How to remain honest in the expression of my love without having any desire to resort to sexual behavior or even imagery. For, indeed, what I feel toward him and want to express cannot be expressed sexually.

Perhaps the Hindus are right. They have a more complex theory of human energies and the body. Where we up-to-date moderns emphasize only sex and aggression, they understand many types of energy playing on our bodies. Sex and aggression, yes, but also tenderness, sheer vitality, purely mental energy, creative energy, contemplative energy.

Nice theory for the Hindus, perhaps, but not too much help for us.

Surely when one is in a significant relationship with another person, there is a play of excitement over our whole organism. We sense a diffuse thawing, a generalized pleasure.

And we don't know what to call it. Not anymore.

So, nowadays, we call it sex.

But though it may, incidentally, sometimes pluck those strings, it is more than and different from. It is not really desire — in the sexual sense — I feel for Wreston yesterday. It is love, tenderness — mixed with admiration, understanding, and even gratitude. But we have no ways of expressing such a mixture to another man anymore.

So dumbly, my smile still on my face, I sit in my chair and feel what I feel. But I do not caress that tired head. And he could probably use it.

One must not exaggerate. This is not a tragedy. We both felt my tenderness. Albeit at a distance. One doesn't have to act everything out. And sometimes silence and restraint are as beautiful as a fond touch. But Wreston and I are more limited than I, personally, would like.

Though the vast majority of the men I spoke with about friendship simply accepted the fear of homosexuality as a barrier, a number took it for some kind of screen, concealing another reality. One saw that fear as really a fear of touching, a fear of all kinds of intimacy. Others claimed that in a tough, alienated society, the fear of all other men's aggressiveness gives rise, in compensation, to vaguely homosexual feelings — which are, in turn, compensated for by the fear. There were even a couple of men who saw homosexuality itself — or rather the militant gay movement — as a compensation for men's affective isolation from one another: the dam of natural love breaks and people are swept away into sex. Such deep theories may have some truth to them, though they are hard to test.

The topic is one of extreme subtlety and difficulty; its exact contours are hard to draw. In any event, one must continue to insist that the importance of sexuality to friendship is easily exaggerated. The anthropologist Robert Brain, after studying friendship in many cultures around the world, comes to the same conclusions:

> Like Santayana I found it hard to accept that sex can be banished from friendship. We have been brought up as "dirty old men," assuming the worst when two men are constantly and devotedly together or when a boy and girl travel together as friends — if they share the same bedroom or tent, they must be lovers. We have imbued friendly relations with a smear of sexuality, so that a frank platonic enjoyment of a friend for his or her own sake is becoming well-nigh impossible. The fact is that sex can be switched on or off as a situation demands — between brother and sister for example — and frequently this favors a more lasting friendship . . . Nobody would deny sex as a source of power behind love, but it is not inevitably nor overtly expressed. More important than carnal urges or "sublimated homoeroticism" are affection, friendship, companionship, and the need to care and be cared for.

Having said this and all the rest, and even after having accepted it, one has not solved the problem — the problem of being true to one's love and tenderness in friendship with a man. The inhibitions on such truthfulness are collective; they derive from the society and are in the air we breathe. Others feel them and draw away. It will help if, together, we begin to accept the obvious idea that in human love sex is not everything. Not even predominant. Sometimes, perhaps more often than one might think, sex is not even involved at all.

11

Women's Lessons

Almost from the beginning, I found myself asking the advice of women about male friendship. First, for many reasons, women often tend to watch men and pay attention to what we do, perhaps with more thoughtfulness than we show toward them. Second, I believed that despite fashionable trends toward women's liberation, unisex, and androgeny, women would be likely to be in better touch with a traditionally feminine element in friendship that had once also been an accepted part of male friendship. Moreover, as many men and women had told me, today is a particularly good time for friendship between women.*

Accordingly, I talked with nearly a hundred women in both America and Europe. Their views varied enormously, of course, depending in part on temperament, age, social class, political per-

---

*Women's friendships have had their cycles. The social historian Carol Smith Rosenberg, among others, has examined these in part. In early-nineteenth-century America, there are records of women's friendships that indicate very close intimacy and mutual dedication. Excluded from a more or less oppressive male society and separated by physical distance, some women left remarkable correspondences testifying to the existence of profound relationships. Then, as women gained more prestige, freedom, and power toward the end of the nineteenth century, these very close, personal relationships tended to die out and new kinds of more social, group relationships replaced them: garden clubs, women's clubs, temperance organizations. The present struggle of women for

suasion, and regional experience and culture. A few interviews stood out as epitomizing some repeated themes, notions I continue to mull over because they are truly challenging if one is looking to better male friendships.

The theme women most often returned to is how contemporary men repress the life of feeling, particularly the old tenderness that used to be possible between men. I particularly recall one woman who put the point with unusual force. Tough, attractive, forty years old, Elizabeth Bacon had worked her way out of the Texas Panhandle conventionality into which she had been born, first to the University of Texas, then on to MIT. She had published, early in her career, several papers on subatomic particles that had a certain importance to a generation of later physicists. Then, without bothering to reap the professional rewards of this early work, Elizabeth had given up the sometimes brutally competitive world of international science to write on topics like women's health and to raise a beautiful young daughter, without benefit of husband. Elizabeth's red hair curling around her head, she looked at me from green eyes with startling boldness and softness mixed.

"It starts when men are very young. I have seen it when I take my daughter to the playground. When the boys are five or six or seven there is a deep tenderness about them. Suddenly, a little later, there is a stage when the young boy has to join the company of 'men,' 'become a man,' and in our society, at least, that tenderness is completely crushed, both by the boy himself and by others,

---

equality, especially in the workplace, has brought them together in new ways and given a fresh impetus to women's friendships.

I was warned by a number of women not to "idealize" the current vogue of friendships between women nor to think that it may be permanent or eternal. One thirty-five-year old director of a famous eastern university's women's studies department is not even sure how "deep and real" the new friendships are. "Even for most feminists, job, career, men, and family all come *far* before friendships." My general impression, however, was that American women had at least better friendships than their men, for the moment, and that we could learn from them.

notably fathers. Look at a father playing with a young boy — it is rough, tough, almost never anything else. Boys stop kissing their parents. They're taught to stop. Most fathers never touch their sons except in roughhousing. How do you expect men to be friends with other men when they can't touch each other?

"I think what happens to the young boy in this situation is that his deep natural tenderness is excised. He offers himself, and at a certain point his trust is rejected. He is toughened up in all kinds of subtle ways. By the time a man reaches his thirties, he is really tired; he is discouraged. In bed with a woman, maybe he can get something, but by thirty-five he has been so often unrewarded. The tender, loving part, more tender than a woman brings, is beaten away.

"What takes its place is fear and fantasy. Fear of other men — of women, too — and fantasy, generally sexual, of some rich play of affection that he can't actually find in life.

"But observe a man with a young girl, a daughter. The man becomes his inner child: he is the child and also himself, at once. For me, it is to see a man at his best. He has his full presence, his height, his sense of self; but it all comes out as vulnerable and tender, and laughing, too. The man is totally unthreatened by this situation. With a young boy, the man's hardness all comes back — the stiffness, the roughness, the increasingly empty performance of manhood."

I feel there is real compassion here, also an implicit demand. Why can't men be more open, more tender? What is one to do, I wonder, simply *get* tender? How the hell does one do that? I close my notebook. We are in the bar of an old hotel in Berkeley, near the university. On the wall is a mural I have seen many times but never really looked at before. The paint has softened its hues with age and there is an overall gentleness about them. The mural is dominated by its depiction of a bronze statue that actually exists on the Berkeley campus, a work from the 1920s or before. Two young men, about twenty-one or -two years old, are shown as football players in the lighter costumes of the days when the game required less armor. One is wrapping a bandage around the calf of the other. The wounded player has allowed himself to sway and reaches out with one hand to support himself on the shoulder of the other man.

There is a certain pastel delicacy about the picture which communicates itself to these muscular men — one allowing himself to be helped, the other careful in his assistance. One has seen the same sway of repose, of relaxed confidence, muscles rounded, in statues of men from ancient times through the nineteenth century. It allows the beauty of the male body to be displayed. We have to — I have to, as I look up at it — call it feminine, and not in any appreciative or even neutral sense. I have to think that the artist, with all that softness of color, of feeling, of posture, must have had some homosexual motive. These reflections only drive home what the woman in front of me has said. Men have been taught to run in shrieking fright from tenderness. I tell myself, we will need real strength to bring it back.

· · ·

Another woman explores complementary aspects of what is missing in men's friendships. Different from the physicist and yet similar, Carla Baselevski has none of the obvious hard will, no hints of longhorn toughness. The Texan was thin and wiry, but Carla looks more maternal, twenty pounds overweight, with hair dyed blond. Carla is older also, nearly sixty. She is a clinical psychologist — her job is caring for others and one expects her to seem different. What both women have in common is an attractive combination of strength and softness. They are the new women. Of course they are the old women, too: the eternal feminine that is receptive and also full of strength and endurance.

"Most of my clients are women," Carla tells me, "but I have noticed the trouble my men patients have with friendships. I have friends, people I have kept from my school days. They are a great ornament to my life: we became someone together. This is very hard to find later. Some women find it, but men have much more difficulty. I think women have a great advantage in friendship. This is because men have such trouble sharing *interests* with other men.

"What is friendship but sharing? But what can men, as opposed to women, share with their friends? The most obvious thing is work. Men are interested in work, of course. But this overriding concern for a job often can't be shared because you have a colleagueship, and that is not the same as friendship. You don't tell *any* colleague all the truth of what you think about work. He is over you, under you, next to you. There is competition. You can't fully trust him.

"Women have a great advantage. Even if they work, by tradition they can share the details of everyday life. Shopping, gardening, decorating, the care of the house, the care of the children. Women can exchange favors in the world of everyday life, without competition.

"Can you imagine a man calling and saying to another man, 'I'm going out tonight, can we leave the children there?' The other man would almost certainly say, 'I'll ask Ann.' Men are supposed to be at work or above all these petty concerns. Get into conversation with a man and he will discuss the great affairs of the world with you, but not the very little intimate details of existence. This sharing among women, especially the sharing of children, is very profound. Now I am even starting to share my grandchildren with my friends.

"Women also share feelings, and we all know that men generally don't do that, though very occasionally they may *talk* about them.

"There is a physical aspect also. Women are allowed to admire one another physically. They can share interests in fashion, in bodies, and they can even say, 'You look great with that new haircut, what a terrific tan, what a suit!'

"Can you imagine men doing that? But, you see, friendship always has *some* physical basis. There's an attraction. You can't imagine yourself being friends, for example, with someone whose smell you don't like. There's a physical affinity. Men are supposed to ignore all this.

"Women also share sex. I mean talking about sex. Contrary to popular belief, men don't really talk about sex. They talk about their fantasies. Women will talk about the reality, not just to a therapist but to each other. They'll say, 'He seems very loving but then he goes limp. I'm desperate about it — I don't know if it's me or him.'

"Ask yourself why men don't talk about sex, why it is hard even to *imagine* it."

She paused for a moment, and I asked myself what she demanded. Her whole approach had been unnerving. Carla was pleasant. Certainly she was not one of those ridiculous but current creatures who were against men. But she was so quietly sure of women's superiority in friendship; it was just a little irritating.

She was right. I couldn't, not right off, at least, imagine men sharing their really intimate sexual experiences — the disappointments, even the pleasures. My mind raced to find a simple reason. I speculated that it could be shyness, or the well-learned lessons that men must perform in sex as they do in work and, therefore, nothing intimate that could give a clue to the quality of the performance, nothing real, even if joyous, could be exposed for fear of possible judgment. Whatever the reasons, it was true. We men have isolated ourselves from this whole aspect of life.

"Let me come back to feelings," Carla continued. She lit a cigarette, her scarlet fingernails flashing over the silver lighter. "I have had many men come in here, sit where you are sitting, and tell me about their childhoods. It has always astonished me how many had very good memories of being with their grandfathers. Perhaps it is because men can express — they are free to express — more of their feelings when they are old. And they are also different, then, about touching. Older men no longer play those violent male games that fathers play with sons. Young men *fight* with their sons. But I have heard men tell me, 'I've got marvelous memories of my grandfather; he would take my hand when we walked; he would sit me on his lap and tell me stories.'

"The last difference I would observe is that women are more inclined to laughter. Men laugh, of course, but usually in groups. It is much rarer to find two grown men alone laughing with heartiness. For me, part of the memory of my best moments in friendship has to do with this intimate laughter — the sharing of the same vision, the same objects of humor. Do you know Ann Arensberg's description of this in her marvelous novel *Sister Wolf?*" She arose, took the book from a shelf, and then, still standing, she explained:

"The two women in this scene are in their early thirties and are coming home from a day's outing. They are both bright Americans, middle class and college trained. The period is about 1958."

They were sitting in the back of the bus coming home from the Regional Cat Show in Pittsfield, making a real teenage scene. They laughed so hard that the driver chewed them out over the loudspeaker: ". . . if those two young ladies would *act* like young ladies." Best friends laugh like that, as if they owned the world, a kind of laughter that is better than sex or back-rubs, and puts heartbreaks and rude awakenings in a long perspective.

She closed the book, looked up at me, and then asked, "*That's* friendship, isn't it?"

I had to nod my agreement.

"And here" — Carla picked a paper out of a file — "is a statement by another literary woman, a forty-four-year-old happily married person, who once came for a few counseling sessions: 'You asked me about my friends. They are like sisters more than friends, but they are sisters without a history (my husband's phrase). We are in touch practically heartbeat by heartbeat, and I think we talk abut our intimate lives more than we do anything else, except books or people. And what I like best about them is they make me laugh. I sometimes wonder what Rick thinks about these surrogate sisters and whether he feels like a parent with a teenaged daughter who ties up the telephone lines all day long.' It's a lovely intimacy, isn't it?"

I nodded again.

"I think this all may change. Men are learning to live with the everyday aspects of life, from housework to child-rearing, and that will give them more to share. Fathers are taking more active roles in raising children. They will touch their sons more, probably be more tender with them. Younger men are more conscious of the lack of feelings in their lives and seem to be determining to be more open. But one doesn't change these deep patterns of withdrawal and avoidance just by wishing it. It will take two generations, at least — this one, and the next — to fully internalize it. Say, thirty or forty years. It could be different then."

• • •

A sad idea but probably true. As I continued to interview women, I discovered a real ambivalence developing within me. Certain of their criticisms and suggestions about male friendship seemed right, but I didn't like the whole process. I found myself, quite simply, becoming defensive. I just didn't want these women to know us so well, to know our shortcomings. Yet, another part of me was glad, took their insights with good cheer, and after searching, found little if any smugness about their suggestions. The women, by and large, seemed compassionate toward our limited lot, as irritated at our self-imposed limitations as I was myself, most frequently astonished and puzzled.

Another woman, an engineer, detailed her bafflement: "Men say, 'Oh, ———. He's a friend of mine.' But you find out he hasn't seen him in fifteen years and what they did was share an office and go out for drinks. In my experience, women are more inclined to be precise about the extent and meaning of their relationships. They will say, 'Oh, we used to work together at Esso' or 'We were in school together,' and 'She's my best friend.'

"It's not just engineers, either: I know a lot of people in the New York literary crowd, the art crowd, the financial crowd — you hear a lot of claims about friendship between men. Talented, successful men for the most part, and rather bright and broad-gauged as men go. As far as I can make out, there aren't any men friends — I mean in the sense that men really know one another. How many times I've had a man say to me, 'Now, you're going to meet my best friend.' Then you see they don't know each other very well: they're not really intimate. I ask afterward, 'Does So-and-so think —— or does he like —— ?' and the answers have tended to be, 'Gee, I don't know.'

"It's not just that men don't talk about their fears with one another — sometimes I think that's all that women friends do talk about — it's just that they don't seem to know the most elementary facts. I find it offensive that so often men seem to be pretending to be friends. Now that I think about it, I feel sorry for them."

An image emerges of women seeing men who are in a hundred ways aloof and don't even know it. One woman, talking about her sixty-year-old psychologist husband, said: "John had a few real active friends up to ten years ago, when he taught at the university in San Francisco. They were also partners in a counseling practice. They really knew each other. They spent eight years in an encounter group together, when all that stuff was new and they were pioneering it on the West Coast. When we moved down here to Los Angeles, it became totally different. John still thinks he has friends, and perhaps he does, but it is I who keep in touch. I remember the anniversaries, I remember the birthdays, I send the Christmas cards, and I arrange for the get-togethers on our vacations. I don't know what it is. Maybe men are supposed to be too independent, or above all of that, or that they are too preoccupied.

She added, "When they all came up here with their wives for a surprise sixtieth birthday party I arranged, John was amazed. He couldn't believe he was loved. I guess that's the advice I would give to men, then, 'Expect to be loved!'"

Now there are many kinds of women in our society: women's libbers and old-fashioned ladies, professional women and mamas, young and old, and various combinations of these and other possible qualities. All of them are different. But over the years I received two main impressions: though many women had their doubts about their female friendships being everthing they would want, they also had much to tell men about friendship — in particular, about intimacy and getting down. Warmth, touch, and feeling, sharing sexual lives, daily mundanities, laughter à deux — such advantages of women in contemporary friendship are repeated to me over and over again. Whatever the limitations of their own relationships with one another, women saw men as thin and insubstantial in their friendships, practically off the ground in their attempts to relate to one another. It was a vision that points the way toward what are, in our time, relatively unexplored aspects of male friendship. I am still not sure what it takes to answer these criticisms — or, better, these perceptions of a lack. But the possibilities are there.

In my own quest, distance from my usual American society had turned me into a letter writer. I was learning, at least, one way to keep in touch. But how to accomplish the rest of what the women seemed to be urging was not as easy and clear. I would continue to ponder on it because it seemed important — some of it, paradoxically, a part of our own "masculine" heritage of friendship we have lost: the "feminine" part.

12

Larry Alexander Returns

Nearly three years have passed since I decided to try to bring friendship with men into my life. While women advise and other men generally deny or lament, I have been carrying my little faith. By letter from Europe, I seek to advance my existing relationships of affection, ones most Americans would describe as already being friendships. It is at once a fighting of gross social currents and a discipline of the heart. Wherever else I look, I see few models. My hopes are not high, but I sustain them out of need and will.

It is at this moment that a man whom I have known for a very long time, an acquaintance really, emerges out of the background of our mutual past bearing the possibility of true friendship. He is a man who kept in touch.

• • •

I was rather different eighteen years ago, an assistant professor of English at Berkeley. Recently out of graduate school, I was trying hard to mold myself to the reflective amenities of an academic career. A part of my duties was to advise fifty randomly assigned freshmen about their proposed courses of study for the following semester. One young man, however, was not the usual bright-faced freshman.

The records told me Larry Alexander was twenty-two, only three years younger than I. Larry's manner had a curious combination of self-assurance and nervous energy. His shiny black hair was combed back in an old-fashioned wave. With his sudden starts of movement, one imagined he had in him a kind of suppressed excitement, like a hipster left over from the 1950s. I was curious.

"You are old for a freshman," I remarked, looking through the dossier.

"I spent three years in the army, in Germany," Larry replied. I can feel his bright brown eyes looking me over. Then he glanced away and began to hum a piece of jazz: "Da-dee-da, da-dee-dee-da . . ."

Though a little startled at the carelessness toward academic decorum, I pursued my curiosity: "How was being in the army?"

"It was all right." He relaxed and slid down in his chair, stretching out his long legs, folding his hands behind his head. "Too much whoring around and getting drunk — but I kept out of the stockade!" Suddenly, his face creased with laughter at his good times and fortune, and I was astonished to see him slap his thigh and double over with his own hilarity. When he stopped, again, rather suddenly, he looked into a space beyond me and resumed humming his jazz tune: "Da-dee-da, da-dee-dee-da. . ."

I retreated into my academic dignity, deciding to take control and do my duty as freshman adviser. I warned Larry not to take the four writing courses he proposed for his first semester. They were all difficult and his grades would necessarily be low, jeopardizing any plans for further studies after college.

"I'll take my chances," he said dryly, "and I don't have any plans. I came to college to learn how to write and that's what I *aim* to do!" Larry slapped his thigh and laughed again.

Perhaps the combination of seriousness about his studies and a total absence of conventional decorum — in those years, students were shy, diffident creatures — intrigued me despite my professorial self. I began to warm to Larry. Besides, there was a certain high-spirited theatricality, a bouncing good cheer, that was attractive, even impressive. But he was also, in his general vehemence, his underbred roughness, a little scary.

As Larry Alexander's studies went on, we saw more of each other. He began taking my courses. That puzzled me because we were so different. Despite his emphasis on the word, his even deciding to major in English, he was deeply nonverbal. He communicated not by words but by his physical presence: by the agitation of his jerky body, by the laughter that seemed so big and subjective, and by an intuitive style of speech that came more from the streets than from books and classrooms. "Know what I mean?" and "You know?" were interrogations that punctuated nearly every sentence. Very often I had no idea at all what Larry meant. Indeed, he seemed to mean some kind of adventurous, self-assertive, antibourgeois madness that was not at all what I had in mind for my own academic self.

"Got so drunk once in the army in Germany, I stole a tank!" He doubled over with laughter. "Too fast for the MPs, though. They didn't see who it was and I left it in a field before they could catch me. Felt bad about it for a few days, could have hurt people. But a man has to live. Know what I mean?"

At the time, I didn't know.

Fortunately, over the four years Larry seemed to calm down somewhat. He read a lot, got good grades. Naturally, his age gave him a real advantage over the younger and less experienced students of literature in his classes. I sent him on to graduate school in English in a good but looser department elsewhere, pleased to think that he was gradually going straight. We lost contact for years. I myself was going less straight: shaken by the events of the Free Speech Movement, I resigned from Berkeley to seek a more active life. Swept up in the momentum of the 1960s, I threw myself first into the abortive reform movement in higher education, then into encounter groups and psychologies, "personal growth," and "humanistic social reform."

• • •

In 1972, out of the blue, Larry Alexander telephoned me. At the time, I was mainly raising money for my own Institute for the Study of Humanistic Medicine, hoping to bring some warmth and understanding back to the overly technical and soulless world of contemporary health care. When Larry asked, "What's happening?" I told him.

He hadn't changed. He related how one night during the Vietnam period, disgusted with his university's politics, he had kicked in the door of the English department and dropped out of graduate school, deciding to take up ceramics. This astonishing turn first away from academia and then from politics was not without its troubles. "I'm pretty good, but I can't make a living. Can't get the capital together to expand my business and sell to stores in quantity. I'm trying to get a small business loan."

Coming from him, I realized, it made no sense. Just as, I saw by then, his majoring in English had never made any sense. Ceramics was too small an art for his expressing himself; indeed, art in general didn't seem to be quite his kind of calling. Filling out enormously long and detailed applications to the Small Business Administration seemed nearly degrading. I was relieved when Larry mentioned that, at least, he had a motorcycle — big and black, naturally.

· · ·

Even in the conventional, wishy-washy sense of the term, we were not friends at that point, just men who knew each other. Despite our ages being close and his extreme worldliness, I had a sort of fatherly feeling for him, left over from the days when we were professor and student. As I look back now, I realize that the inequality of our respective positions was part of what kept us from exploring a friendship.

Of course, we were also separated by our different experiences, temperaments, aspirations, and styles. We just kept missing one another. There was no easy complicity. I never felt Larry understood me and I certainly didn't understand him. When he called again, in 1977, I accepted his lunch invitation. Simply, we had known each other so long now that Larry Alexander had become part of my life.

• • •

Despite my reserve toward his familiar energy, his powerful self-assertion — with more slapping of thigh, more laughter, more flashing of eyes than ever before — Larry fascinated me with his incredible tale.

'I was being beaten by the money game," he began, after the drinks arrived, leaning his face close to mine and striking my glass with his, "and then I decided to beat back!" The usual laughter. "They fucked me over for a whole year to get that small business loan: a lousy twenty-five grand!

"Well, by the time I got it I was disgusted. So I knew this guy in Antwerp, see, from my army days. And he told me where I could get some first-quality diamonds, very wholesale and strictly cash. No questions asked, right? I flew there, put the whole twenty-five Gs down, brought back the diamonds. Two months later I doubled my money, Stuart!" More laughter.

The rest of the tale was a bewildering but fascinating around-the-world adventure filled with obscure phrases about "oil leases," "sugar-cane futures," "land development," "currency speculation," "gold mining stocks," and "bioengineering." A tale of fast buying and selling, fast company and fast airplanes, of quick-witted operations at great risk, sometimes on the edge of the law. In short, thanks to the U.S. Government's Small Business Administration, Larry had become a modest tycoon. He had paid back the loan by the end of that first year and now estimated his net worth at two million dollars.

It was a heart-warmer, the kind of success story that strikes to the very soul of America's fantasy life. But with its enormous risks and all the money he had made, it seemed to separate me from Larry more than ever.

"How you doin,' Stuart?"

I explained that I was doing only fair. I had just divorced. I had turned over my research institute to doctors on my former staff. I had a little money from the sale of my old house and I wasn't even sure what I would do next. For the first time in my life, I told him, I was looking for work instead of work finding me. Meaning and money were both in jeopardy. Naturally, I asked Larry's advice about investments.

"Listen, man. I've got a great deal. How much you want to invest?" This approach was more aggressive that I felt ready for.

I told him timidly — and, let me confess it, suspiciously — that I was the kind of guy who leaves his money in the savings and loan and watches inflation eat it up. Unorthodox investing, even orthodox investing, scared me, especially in the shaken condition of my present life.

"Well, not me, old buddy! Now I just happen to own the oil lease rights on ——." He named a tiny and relatively benign foreign dictatorship. "What we need is capital to survey them. There is no doubt that we will find some oil. You could earn about ten times on your money, say, in a year."

Larry then went into longer explanations, as I posed baffled questions, about "options," "leases," "offshore wells," and a variety of other recondite matters that I could never seem to understand no matter how many times he went over them. He wielded industrial and financial complexities with the dexterity of a field marshal directing an army.

Confused, I hung back.

"Come on, Stuart. This is a *good* deal, as sweet a setup as you're going to see. Why not drop half of what you've got into it and *really* 'start yourself toward financial independence,' as it says in the savings and loan windows?" Laughter.

He looked at me, quietly shrinking away from him, and changed his tone. "Tell you what. I will guarantee that you double your money up to $10,000. You know you can take my word. I'm not trying to sell you anything, you understand. Shit: I've got the whole deal for myself. But you wanted some advice about what to do with your money and *here it is!*" Laughter. "Da-dee-da . . ."

Was he really honest? I wondered. Could I trust Larry with my few precious dollars? This crazy adventurer from another world; what if he was totally wrong about the profitability? Suppose there was an accident and he died? What would his 'guarantee' be worth then? Most important, what could I give him in return? What obligation was I putting myself under? What did I want to do with a dictatorship, however benign?

After a full minute, feeling pressed, frightened, and cowardly — Larry radiated decisiveness and enterprise — I said rather quickly, "It's too risky for me, Larry, too scary."

For a brief moment he looked darkly displeased, but he said nothing more about it. We finished lunch and parted. He said he was concerned about me and suggested we meet in a month's time. I agreed. That afternoon, he was off to buy himself a $300 pair of shoes — tan and white, no less: "Got to look the part of the tycoon!" He laughed as he waved good-bye.

• • •

Over the next few months, Larry called and we saw each other a couple of times. He insisted on buying us expensive lunches, waving aside my attempts at paying the check. From his conversation, I got the impression that he did have a head for business, and that he was scrupulously correct within a code of honor that resembled nothing I knew personally but rather something one has seen in the movies. Everything riding on a handshake and eye contact.

"You see," he explained, "when you are dealing fast, making opportunities and turning things over, you have to have *style*, know what I mean? If you don't, in this kind of fast company, the word gets around and you can find yourself with your legs broken."

Such a world was both exciting and repellent to me. I stopped seeing Larry so often; his visits became annual affairs. He called me every spring to "check in," as he put it.

When I married again and was leaving for Europe with Jacqueline, I had been trying to establish friendships with a number of men. I never considered Larry as a serious possibility. It was then that he pressed on me a new deal — for my own good, naturally. He told me to check it out with a stockbroker.

The stockbroker had never even heard of the field. Either Larry was ahead of his time or this was a big mistake. Nevertheless, after much inward debate, I decided to take a chance with $2000.

"Two thousand lousy dollars!" Larry sputtered. "What's wrong with you, Stuart? This is a legitimate inside deal. You can make a fortune. You know I'm offering you part of my interest — which I worked damn hard to get — a quarter of a million. Listen. I'll guarantee you thirty percent the first year on ten thousand dollars."

I refused. I didn't know how to explain why — the same magma of concerns as before. "Two thousand," said I, holding firm. Larry complied, but he was clearly displeased at what I supposed he saw as mere timidity. I imagined he wished I were more like him, more given to the big risk, more adventurous, more willing to plunge, more likely to get rich — or poor. "I'm not like you," I protested.

"That's all right, Stuart. You go for two thousand." There was, in his voice, the tone of resigned indulgence. For me it was a fortune to put into anything so speculative. The broker had scornfully said, "Think of yourself as putting the two thousand in the ground — there's not much chance of its coming up like a plant! If it fails, it's your contribution to the world." I was a little infected with Larry's reckless playfulness, however, so I put aside all solid business judgment, withdrew the money from my savings account, and sent Larry a check. I made myself do it fast, before I chickened out.

. . .

During the first lonesome months in Europe, the only person who ever called me from America was Larry. Of course, he could afford it. Despite the phone's limitations as an intimate medium, in my isolation from my homeland I was glad to hear a familiar voice, even grateful.

Every six weeks or so the phone would ring, about noon my time, three o'clock in the morning in California. I knew Larry liked the night and imagined him stretching out on the sofa, a drink in hand, wearing a fresh white silk shirt and pressed designer jeans, ready for a long, expansive talk.

Mostly he would ask, "How you doin', Stuart?" After hearing, he would go on to explain the latest machinations and vicissitudes in regard to my $2000 worth of stock. Barely following, I pretended to be very interested. Out of politeness. In fact, I had kissed the money good-bye, as the broker had advised.

I assumed that to a considerable extent, Larry telephoned out of his own loneliness and boredom. Indeed, he once said that it was "great," since he stayed up so late anyway, that he could call people at three o'clock in the morning without waking them up.

. . .

The months passed and I worked on my book, formulating some of the early views and putting them into schematic notes. At a certain moment, I decided to send them off to a number of "friends" for comment and criticism. Though I didn't feel close to Larry, I thought I would pay him back, so to speak, for his phone calls — reciprocate the reaching out, even though I didn't feel like it.

When he called, by chance, a couple of days later, he seemed pleased to be told the notes were on the way. Indeed, he declared with great firmness — the kind of tone he used in discussing business — that he was fully engaged. "I'll read them, Stuart, and then I'll write you and call you about them, both." It was much more than I expected, and the prospect of such a full response meant something to me. Any writer beginning a project wants careful reading. I felt in Larry's voice the solemn energy of a promise from a man whose word was his bond, as they say.

I was very surprised when weeks passed and I didn't hear from him. Weeks turned into a month, then two. With his dangerous style of life, I worried that something had happened to him. Finally, I called, myself.

Two Years and Eight Months After the Lunch with Harry Solano

"Yes, I've read it. I've thought about it a lot. I think about it every day, in fact!" said Larry, a little irritated. "I don't know why I haven't gotten in touch. Can't get my thoughts together, I suppose. Listen, let's make this a short call: I'll write you soon."

I half-smile to myself, thinking I understand what's going on even though he doesn't. I could tell from his tone that he was embarrassed. From my own experience, I deeply understood how difficult it is to deal with the writing of someone you know. You see the writer needs encouragement and help, otherwise he wouldn't ask you to read an unpublished project.

But you don't always like what he sends. It just may not be your cup of tea.

Or you may not understand it.

Or you may sense something wrong but not know what it is or how to correct it.

For all these reasons, you may feel unable to respond frankly. And yet if somebody has turned to you for criticism, you feel you must be honest; for how otherwise can the relationship stay straight? This can all become a minor agony.

"Look, Larry," I say charitably, "don't sweat it." I don't feel easy enough with him to explain what I imagine he's feeling, so I simply tell him, "If you can do it, fine: if not, it's all right, too."

I hope Larry will just forget the whole matter. I imagine he can find a way to evade all the problems connected with responding, and I hope, for his sake, that he will. Besides, I don't really care very much what he thinks — he's really no friend at all. Too different about life from me. I don't think he can be of too much help.

Because he had not written as promised, it was evasiveness that I was prepared for when Larry called again. But Larry was not evasive.

A Month Later

"It's not good enough, Stuart. Oh, I know it's only a tentative sort of outline, but there are real problems with it.

"You have to be more true to the feelings involved. You say you've been keeping a journal but that you're not sure you want to disclose your personal life in the book itself. You've got to reveal yourself. Put it in!"

Larry goes on, stopping only for an instant to remember his next point.

"Sociology and history and literature and anthropology — that background is fine. But the subject needs more guts. It needs to be closer to life. You know what I mean?"

I have to admit that for once I do. It is good advice and I have had some of the same thoughts myself. Only I don't like hearing it.

It means much more work.

Above all, it means making this journal public. I had considered doing that but have not really wanted to. I'm not sure about showing all the back and forth, the eddying and slow comings and goings of my own awkward struggles, the many less than finer feelings of petty resentment, self-pity, loneliness, bewilderment, and disappointment — all part of my search.

And it means the difficult task of finding the exact feeling, tone of subtle inner realities, of myself and others.

Almost as the dread of the assignment pierces me, I find myself becoming strangely elated. As he talks on, he who has hesitated for months to say what he really thinks, I apprehend that Larry is doing something truly special. He is being honest about something that could endanger our relationship: a relationship I suddenly realize *he* values, because — it finally occurs to me — he had gone to real effort to keep it up.

Indeed, until this very moment, when he dared to risk being honest with me, I didn't understand how much he valued it. I am touched, oddly softened, by his taking such a risk — for our sake, for the sake of keeping honesty between us.

Almost as if he reads my thoughts, Larry continues: "I've been thinking about the topic a lot. You raise many questions, more than you answer. And you are right to do so. It is, after all, extremely difficult to create and maintain a real friendship in the world as we find it.

"What one does is create the conditions of feeling in oneself in which a friendship can be maintained. That's the best you can do. And if another person understands, then he'll respond."

An irritation that often overcame me when he talked in his intuitive fashion began to sour the warm feeling I had. But soon Larry makes it embarrassingly clear what he means.

"You know, those deals I have offered, over the last years. For me, the most important aspect was that I *guaranteed* them.

Do you know what that means, Stuart?" he asks. I can feel the memory of angry exasperation fill his voice.

"It wasn't a business deal at all! It was a gift! It was a gesture. That *you* might have followed up on." He stops for a minute, annoyed. "You should have understood that I would never have let you lose money on something I got you into. Never. One doesn't *say* so, of course. Maybe you didn't understand it."

Larry became cheerful and calm again. I can hear the ice being tinkled in his glass. "You're not the only one. I have made similar propositions to other people I like. But even people whom I've done business with," he reflects, "and who have much better reason than you to know how completely trustworthy I am about such promises, shy away from them."

He sounds disappointed. Puzzled, too. But also pleased, relieved, at last, to be explaining himself. As if my having written about the difficulty of friendship in the modern world allows him to speak thoughts that have pained him, in his own aloneness, for a long time.

· · ·

I am shaken.

Yes, of course it was generous. Yes, it was a gift. And yes, I hadn't accepted. And I hadn't trusted him. And I hadn't wanted to feel obligated to him. And I had instinctively drawn back into my own careful, masculine fortress, to calculate for *myself* how much I would be willing to risk on my *own*. To not take anything from anybody, to not get involved, not be bound, to preserve distance, to conduct myself on my own terms.

Perhaps, in a reversed position, had Larry been the poorer one, he would have done the same. He's a male, too, with I assume the same obsession about independence. But that doesn't negate my immediate realization of how simply loving he had tried to be to me. I had missed it and I feel ashamed. Larry is a more powerful man than I had thought. A man stronger in his feelings, his desires and needs for others, in his willingness to risk — with all the tycooning and laughing, and slapping, and expensive shoes — than I had realized.

And he has cared about me in ways I have not appreciated. I just hadn't seen it.

Again, as if he has been able to read my faraway thoughts, Larry goes on.

"Stuart," he says, insistent and still a little annoyed with the memory of my caution and the caution of others in the past, "friendship is like love. It is against reality. It is a necessarily untenable assertion in the face of what the world one knows is. It's something outside of ordinary life. Therefore, it is *better* than life. Both people have to understand that. Anything else is vitiated and determined by society and its usual ways. Anything else is our ordinary existence. It's only when people can step out of their roles completely, the roles their life positions make them occupy, that friendship is possible. You simply have to be a hero."

Moved, but suspicious again despite myself, I take this to be three-o'clock-in-the-morning raving from Larry, glass in hand, beneath the starry California night. Sure, but it is also the truth, one that I, too, deeply believe. That he proclaims it and tries to live it with me — well, it strangely releases me. I soar on the wings of his daring affection. I feel, suddenly, and with so different a creature, not alone. His need is mine. His daring is mine. His insistence, yes, the same as mine. At least in those moments when I am not asleep in what he calls "reality" or "life position."

I force my voice into the silence: "I am very moved by what you have said." My bright noontime diction is so pitifully inadequate to his dark night confidences, to what he has stirred in me, that I clutch the telephone receiver and bend my body forward, as if by such exertions I would lean toward him through the wires and the airwaves. I hope that, somehow, Larry will feel that gesture. "I am very moved." There is only so much you can put into words without making miracles into banalities. The thought occurs to me that perhaps I have already said all that can be said, but the telephone demands more words — gestures, looks, even silences don't count for anything — on this occasion in particular.

"I didn't understand, before. Now, I feel less alone. I am hurt and touched by your daring to be honest about my notes. What you tell me is hard. It is also a gift. And the money, too. I'll have to think about it more — why I refused, then, why it was impossible. I understand, now, what you meant and it counts for a lot to me."

There is silence between us and more than a touch of embarrassment at so much voiced sentiment, out of fashion in our cool times. Then one of us breaks into a more usual tone. We speak of other matters. Our stock deal is a subject to hand. It seems that there's been a problem but he will cover it; my investment is safe. I can stay at his house for as long as I like when I visit California. Et cetera.

Finally comes that period at the end of a long call when you know that the moment has come to stop, to wrap it up. It is all sudden to me. More than I have hoped for. Especially not expected from him. There, in the comings and goings of my own life, I had, by being available to it, at last discovered a true friend who, apparently, had always been just waiting.

Enthusiastic, "I have a friend. We're friends," I say.

Larry has his high standards, also, and moved though he is, he wants to keep them clear. "We're getting there. We're getting there. Listen," he continues, "I *will* write you in detail about my comments."

To me this seems too much for Larry to claim. I know how hard it has been for him to get this far. I insist, "Relax. Relax!

Just Xerox your marginalia and send them to me. You don't have to sweat it anymore. I'll figure out what they mean, or make allowances. It doesn't have to be perfect. Trust *me* a little!"

He laughs. "You got it, Stuart!" I could tell he was grateful for my understanding. "I'll read it again and send a Xerox back to you with my comments on it — say, in a couple of weeks."

After this splendid phone call, I was excited. I imagine a future visit with Larry when there will be much old ground to cover. I imagine some very honest moments. I imagine that I will come to know him in new ways, his having revealed himself this much. Then, despite the enormous differences in our temperaments and interests, friendship might just work. It would take time and some trying, I tell myself, but I have a fantasy that we just might have some very good times together. Just as the phone call was a very good time. I write him about this.

Six Weeks After Larry's Declaration of Friendship

Still no word from Larry.

I don't know what to think. His involvement with me is real enough, his engagement; it is clear that he cares. But I feel a little bit like a fool for taking him at face value. For exulting over his "heroic" friendship toward me. Now I am disappointed, angry that he cannot discipline himself to respond to such a simple request from a friend. Because he cannot seem to find exactly the right comments to make, the perfectly judicious, perfectly helpful, perfectly honest, and perfectly caring response to a friend's efforts, he will procrastinate. His own code of too much excellence, his "heroic" code, his uncompromising idealism, keeps him silent and away from me. This is not *friendly* of him. And I wonder if I haven't, again, idealized someone else's possibilities for friendship. How reliable is Larry? How much can I trust him?

One Week Later

I had decided to be very patient with Larry and wait, but I change my mind today and write him with obvious anger that I am disappointed: "Where is your real loyalty, your real reliability?" Of course, it is a risk, again. But I gamble Larry has enough caring not to cut me off even though I pierce his persona. I also tell him that his silence may only mean *he* has a problem — sickness, troubles, nothing to do with me. I will call him in a few weeks unless I hear from him first.

13

The Circle of Love

While I am waiting for Larry's response — perhaps because of the suspense, the teetering, after so long a search, on the edge of decisive disappointment — other issues come into focus.

Shamelessness, then commitment, come at me through back doors. I need to return to America for a couple of months in order to do research and take care of some business. I write to half a dozen friends: people I have known for a long time, with whom I used to work, or with whom I struggled in the same, now obsolete causes. We have seen each other over the years, eaten many meals together at restaurants and at home, but never, since the time when our professions or the shared idealistic passion for an outside cause bonded us, have we been truly close friends. These are the people I have been corresponding with all these months, building in our mutual imaginations a new sort of presence.

I take what seems a big chance. I ask each if I can stay for a week or so. For me it's a matter of economics, but as Aristotle says, friends are people who "live together." We moderns don't do that much, and I want to live with my friends. I invite them to stay with Jacqueline and me whenever they come to Europe.

Replies come back with gratifying rapidity. By unhappy coincidence, one is leaving for a summer visit to France himself at the

time we arrive in the United States and the apartment has been
promised to others. Another thinks the house is too small for him
and me and Jacqueline together. Most say they are glad to take us
in for the brief visits I ask.

My reactions, as always, unroll and roll back, gradually:
gratitude at their efforts, annoyance that some can't arrange it
(part of me thinks that maybe they could if they cared enough but
they don't, at least not yet). Overall, a warm pleasure.

Six Weeks Before I Return to the States

My state of mind could be attributed to spring. It could be the
warm invitations from America. Even Bob Jones, whose house
was too small, has offered to let us house-sit if we stay so long
that he will be gone on a trip of his own. Wreston "will keep
my eyes open for other possibilities." I realize now I live
within a circle of love. In six weeks, half a dozen people will be
waiting for me on the other side of the Atlantic. I am a friend
and I am befriended.

Or, perhaps, it is due to something more progressive. Something that has been growing underground, like the renewal of
spring itself, for many months. Perhaps it is the accumulated
sum of all my own inner efforts, all the reaching out, the
letters, the yearning toward, the wanting. All the risks.
Perhaps it is the unexpected result of that purposeful holding
in the heart of those whom I would bring closer to me and of
the idea of friendship itself. All that vulnerable caring.

Whatever the causes, if causes there are, I awake today and
while shaving I suddenly realize that I have lost my shame.
The old embarrassment at reaching toward others, at wanting
to put men friends in my life, has essentially vanished. Suddenly, it seems normal to have done what I have. I have always
known that — relied on my classical education, my memories
of Aristotle and Montaigne, of Cicero and Shakespeare, to

reassure myself that friendship was, indeed, normally, humanly, of immense importance. But I have had to fight the modern side of me that said it was exaggerated, weak, childish, unmanly, and above all, unrealistic to care so much for friendship.

That whole shame is gone and I find it perfectly right to do what I have been doing. This is a subtle inner shift but a fundamental one. I never really expected that I would get rid of my inner duality about friendship. How long it has taken and how grateful I am!

Four Days Later

This afternoon, after a late morning's quiet exuberance wandering the sun-flecked medieval nucleus of Brussels, I experience the quiet crash of my good spirits. Yes, there has been much progress but I have not found all that I seek. Yes, I have friends now. They will write to me, they even think about me from time to time, they will let me stay with them, we do favors for each other, we care. But something is missing. What we have is not yet enough. I analyze and ask myself, What the hell is enough? Am I insatiable? What is it I want from friendship? Am I yearning for human satisfactions that only God can supply?

A week later, I interviewed a German filmmaker, a serious and sensitive man, much younger looking than his sixty years. He came to the café prepared with bookmarked texts all about friendship from Goethe and Husserl and Heidegger. He read to me, then he declared himself: "Real friendship in our time is perfectly exceptional. I just finished a two-year film project about men who live together in spiritual communities their whole lives. Even they don't have friends. They don't confide in each other. Sure, they care for each other, but it is impersonal. It passes through God, that caring. We interviewed half a dozen recent entrants, there only three years, for television. They told the camera why they entered, but you could see by the fascinated expressions on their faces as they listened to one another's stories that they had never told each other.

"In men's communities — at least in the monasteries — you don't find friendship. Nor is it readily found anywhere else. You Americans, who so often lead in modern life, seek boundless fraternity! You tell first-time guests to help themselves to whatever they want in the refrigerator, something that makes Europeans shudder. Openness? Certainly. Intimacy? In a way. But not real friendship."

I sensed in his tone an assurance, an authority about friendship that left a still deeper issue to be explored. "You speak of friendship with great certainty," I observed. "Do you have a friend, yourself?"

He regarded me carefully over his glasses. "Yes I do." He smiled broadly. "It has not been simple. We have known each other thirty-two years, though there was a period when we separated. But we have become real friends.

"Our acquaintanceship began in the theater, when we were both actors. We still work together sometimes. I haven't time to describe the friendship and, frankly, I would not tell you much because it is private." He stopped to give the inquisitive American another firm glance. "Even sacred. We are terribly different — he is more volatile, chasing every new idea, new attractions, flighty, even — while I, as you see" — he waved toward the pile of books — "am more serious, inward, contemplative. Nevertheless, we have learned to give each other absolute acceptance, never to try to change one another. Above all, from out of our own inner silence, to *listen*."

"It sounds nice," I said, feeling a mean desire to press him, "but a little ethereal. Do you do more than listen? Would you, for example, mortgage your house for him?"

"No." He answered crisply, almost as if he had entertained such questions himself. "Half belongs to my wife. Besides, I wouldn't do it. I like my house. If what you mean is would I find a way to take care of a massive financial need of his, the answer is yes. We have done more than that for each other.

"The couples are also friends, you know." I sensed a certain pride now, even a hint of repressed boasting. "And when one man has fallen in love with the wife of the other, well, that is a real test. That happened fifteen years ago. We are still friends." He stopped himself, realizing he'd revealed a little more than he meant to.

"How often do you see him?"

"About three or four times a week."

Here is friendship. A relationship that has deepened into a major presence, one in the life of the other. As we parted, he told me, "It is perfectly exceptional in modern life and it takes a lot of time. There wouldn't be room in my life for more than one such friendship." I believed him.

· · ·

While he talked, I compared my own situation with his. I had recently experienced myself as moving in a circle of fondness. This was, since the days of my youth, new. It was a very good feeling to have my American friends in this new way.

I wondered, however, how much real personal commitment we had. Would my friends write to me, if I didn't write? Would they inconvenience themselves, any of them, for me? Would I for them, even? Would we even bother to attend one another's funerals? True, we will do favors for each other when asked. But there is no promise. So weak is friendship in our day — or is it we who are so weak, so bent by the world we live in — that friends do not dare dream of committing themselves in some abstract way, the way people still do in marriage. Friends are accessory figures: if we have time; if nothing else interferes; if we can afford it, financially, emotionally; if our wives say it's all right.

What do we need, then? What does one want? I wanted to know that someone else, besides my dear wife, is really there for me. I wanted a man to know that I am there, too, and that he has full claim on me. I think many men, if they would look inside themselves and dare to feel it, would want the same understanding with another man. At this time I knew, in my own case, a few others were there to some degree. But, we could not be sure of one another.

• • •

Those who say that friendship is totally mysterious, wholly spontaneous, will oppose the very idea of promises in friendship, of abstract commitment. They will argue that commitment must only arise by itself, as it did with the German film director and his friend, following many years and many trials and pleasures. Furthermore, when it appears, it must be unspoken. We know from history that such a position is wrong. Time was when friendship between men came with socially sanctioned brotherhood oaths, literally sealed with blood, and when custom *dictated* mutual assistance, burial and mourning for the dead, taking responsibility for the widow and children of a deceased friend. Some will insist that such involvement in another's life belongs to slower times with different social conditions.

As I wrestled with this issue before my trip to America, I recalled an interview three years before with a twenty-eight-year-old American woman. Working in Los Angeles, she had, a year earlier, made a new friend of another woman her age. Both were talented and promising writers and living on tiny incomes. They filled their separate iceboxes from assignment to assignment, and during the lean periods of free-lancing, they ate sardines and soda crackers and drank water. Both were sensitive, literary creatures, who had to toughen themselves to cover murders and rapes and riots. They would discuss their triumphs and troubles for hours — on the telephone, running in the park, over coffee. The men they lived with admired and resented their friendship by turns and tolerated it because they had to.

These two intense young women, the journalist told me, cared too much for one another and their friendship to leave it wholly to spontaneity. "Starving," as they were, each hoping for the offer of a permanent job on a big East Coast magazine, they still had "agreed not to leave Los Angeles without giving the other at least six months to deal with the departure. So, for example, if I get a job offer, Julie has to have six months, either simply to adjust or to work it out with me, or to find a job in the same city, or for me to reconsider. You see," She concluded with emphasis, "the friendship is really important."

I had to acknowledge that this was not *very* heroic: nothing to the death, not one for all and all for one. But for modern, hard-pressed, young career women, it was a pact, a promise of something. For their friendship, the women were willing to pay the price of commitment.

Three Months After Larry's Declaration of Friendship

Larry Alexander and I have no commitment about the slightest aspect of our friendship. In fact, he still hasn't answered my letter complaining about his failed promise to send me his annotated Xeroxes of my early notes.

At last, poised to run with disappointment, to fight with anger, I telephone.

Larry spaces "Hello, Stuart" far apart. His hesitating voice is full of darkness.

"You're pissed off at my letters?" I suggest.

"No." He hesitates but, always forthright, admits hurriedly, "I haven't read your letters." Silence.

I'm amazed, puzzled. I wait.

"I've had some fucking obsession about your letters. I haven't opened the last two. They lie here like talismans."

"Is there anything else wrong?" I ask. "Are you all right? I've been worried by your silence."

"Yes, I'm all right." he snaps.

"Your financial affairs O.K.?"

"Yes, my finances are fine."

"Your relationship with Sherri going well?"

"Yes."

"But you're feeling crazy about my letters?"

" 'Crazy' is the word."

Paradoxically, I am touched again. I think I understand. Quite practically, with the international phone minutes ticking by at five bucks each from the European end, I decide to fill his silence and to comfort him:

"It's fine, you know. You just take friendship very seriously, that's all. I don't know *exactly* what you're feeling, and it's clear from your tone and what you say that you don't either. But you were so upset by the original material on friendship, more engaged with it than anyone else who saw those notes, that I can't help but think you're just a particularly old-fashioned type. Personally, I think you're right to take friendship so seriously. It involves most of the important concerns of life: loneliness, death, love, succor, comradeship, understanding."

Larry just listens, letting me speak into his confused but charged silence. Though his stillness makes me feel awkward, I decide to go on a little bit more, to snap him out of his paralysis.

"Don't let it worry you. In Russia, all the feeling you are having about my book, about the subject of friendship, about our friendship, would be considered normal. Not crazy. In America, too, in the nineteenth century."

At last, in his old way, Larry laughs at my little speech. Then, his voice more full, less restrained than at the beginning, he mocks our shared seriousness: "Well, gee, Stuart, you almost make me *feel* normal."

"Well, neither of us is *normal,* Larry." We both laugh. "You just put those letters away for now and take it easy. You can open them in front of me and we can talk about it together. I'm coming in two weeks."

As we said good-bye and hung up, I thought again that Larry and I had no commitment yet. But there was a degree of involvement implied by his intensity toward our relationship that continued to give me courage. In the next few weeks, I would find out about my other American friends and about him. I realized, after our conversation, that I was heading toward whatever fulfillment three years of trying to take friendship seriously might, for the moment, provide.

14

The Possibility
of True Friendship

Three weeks after visiting old friends in the United States, I abandoned my journal about friendship. I was too busy living my subject.

Those first weeks were full of meetings with the half-dozen people with whom I had been involved for years — Wreston, Bob Jones, and others. Full of the pleasantness of reunions, much American warmth and informality, hospitality, old acquaintance. There were the gradual recognitions (after sudden barking) by guardian dogs one has known and by whom one has been momentarily forgotten, laughter over remembrances, and the happy proffering of new or grown children for examination, caressing, judgment. After being away for so long as a year and often bereft of the sociableness that passes in most modern minds for friendship, I felt myself flooded with good feelings, support, exciting exchanges. The busy round of luncheons, cocktails, and dinners; the cheery and felt hellos, the eager inquiries about details of my year, were all gratifying. It was much more than I had imagined or, indeed, been used to before my year away writing to friends, holding them in my heart.

• • •

Larry Alexander was supposed to pick me up for lunch. As he walked in the door of the house I had borrowed in San Francisco, I experienced that mingled happiness and fear one has when a tall, handsome, nearly strutting male makes his entrance. I had been sitting at the desk in the front room puttering with papers. He had seen me working through the window, rapped, and opened the unlocked door. He strode in, stopped just short of me, looked down, and extended his arm in a strong but distant handshake. Larry was confident and beaming but streetwise. I remembered his telling me that he always conducted himself "a little careful."

Larry's vitality, however, is contagious. I pick up my jacket and kiss Jacqueline a quick good-bye. She looks at us shyly but appreciatively, the woman's knowing savoring of male energy. Quickly, we head down the front steps, all bucking knees and heavy footfalls. Descending, our eyes watching where our feet are going, he palms me a roll of green bills and says, "Three thousand dollars, Stuart! Your share on the stock deal." Thirty hundreds suddenly in my hot hand, knees still bucking down stairs, I understand instantly that it is his natural style. Intended to be a little dramatic, certainly, but more than that: no banker's checks, no cold official papers, just personal, friend-to-friend cash. The air outside smells fresh, and before I ask the dozens of questions about the deal — the troubles in the market, if he wasn't just doing me a favor, and what I might owe *him* in return — I just relish the strong moment. Trust and verve and dash and gratitude. I like it. I like it. It is a hard-won simplicity.

. . .

Over the next few days it is curious to me, from past telephone calls, the unopened letters, the seriousness with which he has taken the business of reflecting on friendship, how we have suddenly become close. My old fear of Larry is gone, and with it, also, a certain distance he has felt toward me.

There is wonder, too. For during our chatty reunion meals I

am less concerned with the future possibilities of our relationship than with the wonder of who Larry is. First came my thousand-dollar profit on a risky investment. To be sure, I earned it. But he had been willing to cover it, as he told me, in case of loss — a gift. (I am thankful we didn't lose; otherwise I would have had to deal with his giving me the money back, and that would have come too early for me in our growing understanding of one another.)

I mention that I want to show Jacqueline Yosemite Valley.

"Take my car."

"You can't mean it," I say, astonished. Some part of me still the old mentor, I admonish and protest. "That new Jaguar!" He was clearly not thinking the act through. I call his attention to the obvious: "You know that anything can happen to a car — vandalism, hit and run, engine blowup —"

Not even smiling at the little lecture, Larry interrupts. "It's all right. I'll take complete responsibility. Besides, I know you like good cars and I think you'll get a kick out of driving it."

So simple. And generous.

That is the way Larry is. In his newly built house, I admire a six-foot but minutely elaborated ceramic sculpture — the abstracted form of a woman, with whole navies of galleys, hundreds of minute oarsmen, complete with tiny oars and bucklers, and dragons and maidens, rich treasure and flowing grasses, all pouring from every orifice in the plenitude of the divine mother goddess. An astonishing, joyous, daemonic tower of fruitful detail that, mounted on a tall dais, reaches upward to the tall ceiling.

I ask who did it.

"A friend of mine."

I ask Larry how he managed to move it without breaking the hundreds of tiny, fragile details.

"My friend and I pack it up, very carefully, each time I move, put it in a hired pickup, and drive it from place to place at five miles an hour. The other drivers behind us go crazy, but I've never broken one of those tiny arms!" He laughs. "In this house, I had that big lighted space built for it. I like it very much. I'm glad you do, too."

Larry loves the piece and the man who did it. "This guy is so obsessional and so into what he does that he forgets to eat, or even to work to eat. So I gave him ten thousand dollars. When he finished it, he gave me the statue."

The niche in which the statue sits, with its own large skylight, is also a subject of patronage. I ask who designed the house. The statue looks perfect in the space it occupies.

"My old college roommate, Danny, is an architect. You remember him from Berkeley, maybe. You know how hard it is for architects these days. I gave him the commission for the house — we worked on the design together. It's a good investment for me, of course, and gives Danny a chance to show his stuff to future customers."

, • •

Slowly, from details let drop and other leads into which I inquire, Larry emerges as a man who, despite the often frenetic pace he must maintain in his business dealings, finds time for an attentive and remarkable generosity. My former Berkeley teaching assistant, Roswell Angier, now a master photographer of the human scene, has also received a grant of ten thousand dollars to pursue his artistic life. Larry shows me Roswell's bitter and beautiful photographic essay on the Indians of Gallup, New Mexico. At one point, I mention that my nephew on faraway Long Island has a new speedboat he wants to show me.

"Maybe we can all go on mine here," replies Larry. "I've got one, though I never drive it. Got it as collateral for a bad loan to a friend."

"Where is it? Who keeps it?" I have seen no signs of boats or the accompanying paraphernalia one usually expects to find in garages or sheds.

"Oh, these people I know keep it for me and do the maintenance; I never use it myself but they get to use it."

I begin to comprehend: Stuart gets the Jaguar to go to Yosemite, Danny and Roswell the grants, and these other characters the speedboat. Gradually, I learn that a daughter by an early, failed marriage, after being with her mother during Larry's many poor years, lives in a suite in the new house. She has a sports car. Larry's girl friend has moved in with *her* daughter. As the days pass, I ask more questions, my curiosity growing with my admiration. Larry's mother, who used to be a supermarket checker, has been bought a new house on a Southern California golf course. His stepfather — even though a brute, in the past, to both Larry and his mother — has received a dry cleaning business.

Many people make money, but few, in my experience, use it in ways so full of heart. Larry doesn't brag. My old dead-end kid even makes some attempt at hiding his generosity. But he is, quite humanly, unsuccessful at doing so. Besides, a friend of his can't help but discover it.

There is a true largeness of character in such magnanimity. The Greeks and Romans held this to be the primary of the pagan virtues. What touches me is his expansiveness wedded to taking care. Larry takes care of people. It goes with the seriousness with which he read the notes for my book.

• • •

Larry and I talk, several times, about friendship. One day he begins to speak of the betrayals of the past. "People," he remarks a little grimly, "will reveal, one time or another, whether they have the heart for friendship or not."

He recalls a high school buddy who was "really careful" with his car. "Well, I needed a car for dates. Life was impossible in Los Angeles without one. This guy had a car. So I asked to borrow it one time, as I had before. We're driving along, him behind the wheel, and he says, 'You need me. You need me to drive you here and there, to lend you my car. So you listen to me and do what I say, understand?'

"I told him to let me out at a gas station. He wanted me to get back in, but I told him to drive on."

"Was that the end of it?"

"Yeah, that was the end of it. I saw him in Berkeley, years later. But I never considered him a friend after that. Or even a prospect for a friend. Know what I mean?"

I did.

"Were there other betrayals, after childhood?"

"Of course. And they were not only more adult, Stuart, they *hurt* more!" He laughed, for a moment, in the old way. "I knew this guy, met him at college. A struggling poet who had become a doctor. He wanted to be William Carlos Williams in the country. A serious guy, he pioneered home childbirth when not a doctor near Santa Cruz would touch it. He could have been a brain surgeon and made a lot of money, but he wanted to help people more generally than that."

Even now, though he had told me the friendship had turned out badly, Larry still spoke of the poet-doctor with the respect, the admiration, that is the basis of much of men's love for one another.

"I can't go into details. Let's just say that once my life was in danger. I needed medical help. If there was a slip-up, then this guy, if he helped me, could have gotten into trouble, maybe with the law, certainly with the local medical society. Rather big trouble. He refused me. And I knew we would never be friends again."

"You mean that you rejected him because he wouldn't put his life and career in danger for you?" I was beginning to wonder just how exigent Larry's standards of friendship might be.

"Shit no, Stuart!" Larry looked at me with the indulgence one must grant to someone still getting to know you after eighteen years of acquaintance. "No, I could understand that. He had two kids by then, a wife, and had become essential to his little country community. It was just that he sent me away to find another doctor without *telling* me it cost him dear to do so. He wouldn't let himself suffer for refusing a friend, for choosing himself and family over me, even for being afraid of the legal and professional consequences. Do you get it? He was *cold*."

Once again, I got it.

He continued after a silence. "Well, I have seen that happen to a number of people over the years. They get gripped by their professions, their families, and they just kill everything else. Afraid even to feel. Hell, I know that not everybody can take the risks I will. Not everybody is built that way. But I can't let them betray me in their hearts. I can't live with people like that. It hurts me a lot that so many people feel they have to kill their fires that way, that completely."

• • •

I was moved. Not only by the depth of Larry's feeling and his continued openness to friendship. He also impressed me because he was the first man I had talked to, the only one among all the hundreds of men I'd interviewed, who had spontaneously raised the notion of betrayal and its pain. Of course, other men had had the experience, but they would never, spontaneously, discuss it. The man has emotional courage.

• • •

"Why didn't you open my letters?"

We were seated on the terrace of the Alta Mira Hotel, looking at the sailboats on sunny San Francisco Bay. My two letters, from months before, were in Larry's hands. Before he opened them I wanted his answer.

"I read the notes for your book five times. I had lots of thoughts and lots of objections." He hesitated. "But I hadn't been able to discipline myself to do a systematic critique." His voice hardened even more. "It was difficult. I had made notes of my own on *your* notes: They took me an hour a page." He spoke haltingly. "I don't know why, that's what they took. I'd lay up at night thinking about what to say and it didn't seem very good. So, I never got it together. I was ashamed and embarrassed. And I had other things to do. If I didn't do it exactly right" — he looked out now over the bay toward the far hills, rather miserable for the instant — "I'd endanger our friendship. Finally, I didn't want to hurt myself again by opening the letters."

"But Larry, I had let you off the hook. I had told you any old comments would do, that I needed whatever you could give me, even if it was second rate, at that stage, and even if it was clumsily put, or inaccurate, incomplete, foolish."

He nodded. "It's easy to say." Regret mingled with defiance and shame; then he took his unused steak knife and sliced open both envelopes. That was all there was to it. He nodded at the contents of the letters, already largely discussed. I could see that he appreciated my understanding of him in them, despite the annoyance and even the pain his own turmoil had caused me during those months. The bond between us strengthened.

• • •

Over the next weeks I see Larry every few days. As personalities, we come up against each other in varied situations — in restaurant talks, at his house, driving. We even go to Tahoe — just the two of us — for a couple of days. I watch him gamble in the plush honky-tonk atmosphere. He cruises the casinos looking for "a blackjack dealer that looks right," flicking his chips, sauntering, betting with intense though careless-seeming attention. Mostly I just watch. My impressions of him deepen. I see in Larry a talent for living, something I had always felt, I suppose, from the first crackling energy when he walked into my office. Then, I could only draw away. It was too alien to my professorial self. But Larry's sense of adventure, his verve, his wisdom, and above all, his deep yearning and caring for people — his need for them and his kindness — I had missed that, too. Not just the more spectacular qualities, even the sweet kindness I had missed. Such obtuseness over such a long time was not really like me.

Larry shrugged when I raised the point. "You didn't miss anything, Stuart. I just wasn't showing much. How could I? When you are trying at life and remorselessly failing, as I was then, one is not very interesting. At the least, being the kind of person I am, you don't really show yourself under those conditions. Nowadays, of course, things are different." He laughed.

So Larry's success had let him come out, and I was grateful.

Where our friendship will go from here, who can tell? Life is so full of chance and, still, he and I are very different. Jacqueline noticed a change the other day that gives me confidence in the future.

"You're imitating him."

"Who?"

"Larry, of course."

I looked puzzled.

"You are unconsciously imitating some of his mannerisms — just a little bit — the strutting walk, humming to yourself. Often you laugh like he does."

I could see, as soon as she said it, that she was perfectly right. It pleased me.

Indeed, after a moment, I laughed aloud with pleasure. It is a familiar experience, though not a recent one. When you start to love someone, you take him into you. You unconsciously take parts of his being and, with them, some of the outer appearances, the manners that are the symbols of deeper realities. I remember how I always used to do this with close friends, when I was a boy, in college, and maybe for a while after that.

Later, with men at least, this automatic absorption of the other had ceased. Indeed, I purposely helped to kill it. I don't know exactly when it was, but at a certain moment, somewhere in my mid-twenties, perhaps, I found myself imitating someone's smile, or laugh, and I deliberately stopped myself. Establishing my own identity had, by then, become overwhelmingly important to me, much too important to chance letting another person in.

It is a stage of hardening the self that all men go through, part of the journey from child to man. It is probably necessary and certainly in our society inevitable.

Now, I see, I have arrived at another stage, one where I've got more identity and independent manhood than I can quite stand. This spontaneous, unconscious opening to Larry and his mannerisms — many of which I rationally consider rather odd, silly, unattractive — freshens me. I am proud of it. Proud that I can, so literally, let another man into myself that way. It means that at a deep level there's still some real life left, some innocence.

Above all, I notice that in myself and other men, giving up the search for male friendship is the result of an end to all innocence. Ferruccio, that old, cool-eyed aristocrat, makes it clear. The leavings, our own and those of others, the misunderstandings and outgrowings, all take their toll, and we, even in little ways, close up. As Larry said, "People are afraid to feel."

To close up so much is to die in the heart. A cynic would say that conserving some of our innocence is, therefore, an illusion necessary to true maturity. Let the cynic put it that way. For the moment, at least, I say that innocence revived is the freshening rain of life on dead and wintered fields. One is, of course, still adult, grown up. One's eyes have been opened by life. I look at the prospect of a serious male friendship — at last offered — with a new awareness, judgment, and prudence. But the innocence, the necessary innocence, thank God, is back in my life, even into the bones and muscles of my ridiculously imitating body.

15

In Lieu of
a Conclusion

E. M. Forster once explained the impossibility of giving a rounded and conclusive finale to novels. They are so close to life, he observed, that one cannot really end them. Life is a continuing process. Without the overused devices of death and marriage, he wondered what novelists should do.

Like life and novels, the search we have followed here cannot be concluded. I wish I were able to depict me and a true male friend — Larry, Wreston, or Bob Jones — riding off into the sunset. I wish I could give you a formula for the general reconstruction of male friendship as a vital social institution. Instead of answers, our examination has more often provided painful and urgent questions. I hope these questions have helped to strengthen men readers, to shake men out of their deadening self-isolation, their programmed obsession with work and achievement and personal growth, timid lack of commitment, and learned fear of intimacy — on all of which the state, the corporation, and various other organizations of modern life prey.

The quest for a place in modern, urban, post-industrial life where deep male friendship currently exists seems for the moment exhausted. My personal quest has reached a certain fulfillment and contains promise for more.

What then has been learned about the nature of true friendship? Was my quest worthwhile? If so, what can be learned from it? What advice do I, after such a long journey, have for others?

In the preceding pages, I have tried not to simplify or idealize. The complexities of friendship — the longing, the embarrassment and shyness, the stiffness, the excessive excitement over small gestures of caring, the easily bruised feelings, the resentments, the shame, the guilt, even the boredom — have all been noted. After all this, I declare that true male friendship, the kind that very, very few adult men in America and Europe have with one another, requires intimacy, complicity, engagement, and commitment. It is a relationship profoundly personal.

Intimacy, being at ease, being understood and understanding, one can find more frequently in modern life than friendship, now that a growing informality of manners and an acceptance of a certain emotional expressiveness have definitively signaled our difference from the more repressive aspects of nineteenth-century social life. Indeed, a dozen modern interests contribute toward moments of intimacy — from psychology, psychotherapy, and encounter groups through nostalgia for the proletarian and the natural or rural, through the cultivated casualness of the modern workplace, to experimentation with drugs and involvement in political and religious movements. The same tendencies promote the increasing occurrence of moments, however fleeting, of complicity, a feeling of secret understanding and even of revolt or secession from society and from wearing our normal social personae.

Friendship between men may be on its way back. Indeed, from younger men one sometimes gets the impression that they are determined to maintain male friendship in their lives. The recent proliferation of popular books on the subject of friendship in general, despite their oversimplifications and lack of feeling, give further evidence that a renewal of male friendship may be preparing itself somewhere in the collective unconscious.

Intimacy and complicity, however, do not by themselves make friendship. Even familiarity — cosiness and trust and occasional supportiveness — can be mistaken for friendship. True friendship must also be true engagement with the friend — a very frequent mutual holding in the mind and heart. Though the centrifugal pressures of modern life limit the frequency of the physical presence of friends, engagement makes physical proximity less of a problem. Male friendship can thus be thought of as a place in a man's inner being, a space in his life, that is daily occupied by another man, a place that is regularly charged with love, concern, thoughtfulness — and, sometimes, resentment, anger, even deep hurt. *Engagement* means emotional involvement.

True friendship implies commitment, the understanding that a friend will be there, will not let go, that a friend will maintain the engagement in the face of obstacles, misunderstandings, and temptations, that a friend is prepared to undertake inconveniences, even sacrifices.

A true male friendship is personal. The relationship is its own context. Friendship may arise from another relationship — work, for example — but it is not dependent upon it. Male friendship is just one man and another. That so many friendships break up or attenuate into nothing when common place, interest, or work are no longer shared means that men have not had the essential friendship.

If a man changes religion or political belief, that does not change an essential friendship. The friends have been truly involved with each other, not just with parties, organizations, or even, extreme as it may seem, with mutual ideas or interests. All these other elements have their own value and importance, but from the point of view of male friendship, they are merely the furnishings, at most a supporting context, tools for the friendship.

A man's high-voltage engagement with another man, each of whom has a daily place in the other's inner being — from such

inwardness, all necessary, dignified, and pleasant actions can grow.
That's male friendship.

And, yes, it is rare.

. . .

My personal quest for a true male friend, though often a painful
struggle and still incomplete, has been worthwhile. I have an instinctive sense that someone else's quest, in the same direction but
perhaps following other ways, would be worthwhile too.

Out of my quest has come a leap in the intensity of older and
more casual relationships. The kind of relationships most would
call friendships but that, in fact, had not had very much intimacy,
commitment, engagement, complicity. They originally arose out
of past involvement in something other than each other. Mysteriously, however, nearly half a dozen people I have known fondly
but not really well have abruptly moved closer to me and me to
them. We are not yet, and probably never will be, the deepest
friends that I wish, but we are still suddenly much closer.

This reward is hard to describe. Because the emotional involvement is not of the highest, it doesn't easily lend itself to
dramatic depiction. For example, a lawyer friend and his wife,
people I had known only slightly but had always felt a certain
fondness for, absolutely insisted that Jacqueline and I spend a few
days with them. This is certainly a measure of some real trust, and
liking, and a desire to show they care. The accumulation of such
gestures filled me with a sense that life was subtly richer, more
secure, less alone, more sacred, even, than it had been before.
Suddenly, I found myself wanted and given to in ways people
don't usually bother with in our modern age, where everyone is
supposed to take care of himself and be on his own. This is not the
highest type of friendship, but it is a lot more than the normally
modern and bureaucratic lunch or dinner date.

If I try to analyze the mystery of this suddenly increased closeness, I would have to say that the single most important contributing factor is that I have given myself to these people in many little ways. Equally important, however, is my having made a big deal about the whole matter of friendship. I have talked whole evenings long about male friendship with friends, corresponded about my thoughts, told of the decay of friendship as an institution, related what you have read here. Perhaps, only dimly aware of it, I was issuing people a challenge to look at our casual relationships, to recall the fuller meaning of friendship, to care. Perhaps, from another point of view, all these discussions merely provided, for once in our contemporary life, a type of social matrix for male friendship, a shared arena in which the myth of male friendship could reassert itself and be attended to. The effect has been to raise the collective ante. Men have had to judge our relationship — indeed, all their relationships — by the usually neglected standards of true friendship. They have had to choose, sooner or later, whether to stay where they are or to move closer to me. Many have moved closer.

This increased intensity has also given me new respect for the several levels on which friendship is possible. Before, the superficiality of most friendships made me insist that only the real thing would do. I could have no respect for men who glibly asserted that different friends had different meanings in their lives, that a middling level of male friendship was, after all, natural and life enhancing. Generally, I still have no respect for such assertions. They are often excuses for promoting the superficiality of most current human relationships. Now that some men I know have become clear, together with me, about the real difference between genuine friendship and everything else that goes by the name, an intermediate level of male friendship has formed itself which, surprisingly, has its own authenticity. By no longer kidding ourselves, homogenizing every fond relationship into an indiscriminately general friendship, some of my male friends and I are able to exist for one another, clear eyed, in a middle distance that has more engagement than before. This middle position, a product of greater hard-mindedness about what male friendship is, is expressed subjectively by more tenderness, by firmer and keener looks, and also by a generalized sense of the opening of possibilities: a sense that perhaps we can gradually explore more fully the true meaning of friendship between us. Objectively, it is expressed by a greater concern with physical welfare, a willingness to do mutual favors, a commitment to correspond, mutual invitations and agreements to visit and live together. With Larry, of course, I have moved even farther: we are on the brink of a deep friendship. In all justice, I have to call these results reward enough for the difficult quest.

I say to others, "If you can stand the quest for a true male friend, it is worthwhile." Each man will find his own way, but I have some brief advice.

In our times, we must first truly accept the necessity for an art of male friendship. Though Willie Morris makes his point about friendship being a grace that one receives, it is not generally sufficient to await the coming of such a gift. Why even those who most strictly speaking seek grace are always busy trying to get what they know can only be given by God. As talented artists who are busy working away at practice and execution, so must friends be diligent. Without deliberately focusing on my need for male friendship, I would have continued to miss Larry — both who he is and his availability for friendship. I have met many people who claim that friendship must be "wholly natural," that it must "just happen to you," and that "it can't be meditated or forced — that's too cold-blooded!" Believe me, there is nothing cold-blooded in thinking about love, about those we love, and in giving and seeking love.

This is especially true in our own cool and changing world. While a whole gamut of human relationships were "natural" in some older societies, they are no longer so in modern urban life. No type of human relationship is a given anymore, is seemingly "natural." Morris and others who plead for simple naturalness in relationships are not new voices. But just as couples these days must work at — indeed, continually reinvent — marriage and child-rearing, men must, if they are to have it, work at male friendship.

What makes a deliberate approach to friendship so necessary now is that everything in our culture is against it. Paradoxically, to keep up one's attention and effort, one must remain continually conscious of the formidable obstacles to committed, intimate, engaged, and personal relations. Ferruccio discussed some of the opposing forces: the calls of work and family life, the squeeze of time, the cynicism that comes with aging. There are, as we saw earlier, many others. The list is endless and every person should add to it. It is good to look your enemy in the eye.

Bold acts of consciousness are, I think, the true basis for an art of friendship these days. No gimmicks will work. The arts of friendship we need are inner acts, acts of the depth of the heart, of self-searching, and of decision.

Inwardly accepting the necessity to give friendship one's closest attention and recalling the social obstacles to friendship are the two basic inner acts.

Others are:

Being willing to acknowledge the hurt of your own loneliness. We live in a lonely time when no one is alone. Our mobile conditions give most of us an enormous but shifting and, therefore, superficial acquaintance. Let the reality of your loneliness be a spur to your own authentic quest.

Being shameless in thinking, then talking, about male friendship because it is important. Make room for friendship in your life. Make a federal case out of it.

Being willing to be hurt, repeatedly, by people you befriend.

Being persistent. People will back away from you, frightened because they have been hypnotized by society into believing they haven't the time, the energy, the interest, to be friends. They are simply not used to friendship anymore. Bizarre as it may seem, deep friendship strikes them as bizarre. Keep coming.

Committing time to friendship: time for writing letters, for thinking about friends, for telephoning friends, for disappointments, for generous acts.

Acting forthrightly with your friend and with the courage of your own delicate needs and desires by living the openness, generosity, and commitment you want from him. You thus help create an example, a magnetic field, in which (with luck) a man may respond. Friendship may arise.

A cunning hint: be willing to ask your friend for favors, to take, to sacrifice a part of your independence.

One hope: the art gets easier. Gradually, you give up the shame and embarrassment while still retaining an essential vulnerability.

After all such art, pray for grace.

• • •

Personal initiatives, however, will not be wholly sufficient. The fact that male friendship is as dead as it is requires collective action. So often in the personal quest for friendship, thinking a lack of a true male friend is a problem to solve alone, a man finds himself feeling crazy. Jung puts it well:

> A collective problem, if not recognized as such, always appears as a personal problem, and in individual cases may give the impression that something is out of order in the realm of the personal psyche. The personal sphere is indeed disturbed, but such disturbances need not be primary; they may well be secondary; the consequences of an insupportable change in the social atmosphere.

The current social atmosphere renders true friendship between men very difficult. When you decide to take male friendship seriously, to make it a real presence in your own life, then you and I both have a better chance of succeeding at our friendships. Our behavior seems, again, more natural, and we take courage from one another.

Let courage then be the word to close upon. A Frenchman, about sixty years old, gray-haired, wiry, and distinguished, one who had ridden his cavalry mount to the front to face the Nazi tanks invading France only to be compelled to retreat in shame, tried to put the whole matter of friendship in brief perspective: "Of course friendship is dead now. There was a time, and I remember my father talking about it, when men had other images in their minds about how to behave. Men were supposed to be steady, to adhere to heroic codes, to keep their word, and to be willing to sacrifice. One learned it by example in many families. My father taught me that one should behave in life with 'honor and elegance.' That was almost all the advice he had to give me. But such talk seems absurd now, doesn't it, because we have become a people of sellers and buyers. Our attitudes toward human relationships are those of supermarket shoppers: we want what is cheap and quick and easy; we want variety; and we want novelty. But friendship requires a whole other set of mind, doesn't it? Commitment, courage. . ."

Recently, as I have become convinced that Larry Alexander is really available for friendship with me, that he is capable of or, at least, that he may be willing to commit himself to our friendship, I have felt a paradoxical emotion. I have been seeking a true male friend for so long and, at last, here is a possibility. Yet something in me draws away from Larry.

Puzzled, I attend to this feeling. To my dishonor, I hear within me a seductive whispering, a little inner beast posing the questions that dissolve all manliness: "Are you sure you want to get this involved? Do you think you can afford to take on another person? What if he makes demands of you: he gets sick, he loses his money?"

This reflexive cringing from all true engagement is a curious emotion. Probably it is part of human nature, the instinct of self-preservation asserting itself, a deep suspicion of involvement with others, of involvement with anyone outside myself. A reaction known even to our most ancient poets.

To meet such fears, only courage will do.

Oh Gods! Let me have the strength and the courage to love my friends!

— Pindar's prayer

Further Reading

There has been a great deal published on friendship, and a recent increase in writing on the subject. The number of magazine and journal articles in the United States has tended to double every five years in the last fifteen. But most recent writing tends to be superficial and heartless, taking for granted the sunken status of friendship in particular and relationships in general. Many other works suffer from a naive, almost gooey hopefulness or from a shallow moralism, a bootstrapping ruddiness that would pretend we can have simple and noble friendships just by keeping our hearts pure and our noses clean.

With this warning, I offer the following list of books to assist the reader's own search. I have starred four titles that provide hundreds of additional bibliographical references from anthropology, psychology, philosophy, and literature.

Allan, Graham A. *A Sociology of Friendship and Kinship.* London: Allen and Unwin, 1949.

Arensberg, Ann. *Sister Wolf.* New York: Knopf, 1980.

Ariès, Philippe. *Centuries of Childhood,* translated by Robert Baldick. New York: Knopf, 1962.

———, and Françoise Dolto. *Enfance, histoire, psychoanalyse.* Paris: Scarabee Editeurs, forthcoming.

Aristoteles. *Aristotle on Friendship, Being an Expanded Translation of the Nicomachean Ethics, Books VIII and IX,* edited by Geoffrey Percival. Cambridge: Cambridge University Press, 1940.

Avedon, Burt. *Ah, Men!* New York: A & W, 1980.

Bacon, Francis. "Of Friendship." In *The Complete Essays of Francis Bacon*. New York: Washington Square Press, 1963.

Bald, R. C. *Literary Friendship in the Age of Wordsworth*. New York: Octagon, 1968.

Bate, W. Jackson. *Samuel Johnson*. New York: Harcourt Brace Jovanovich, 1979.

Battalia, William O. *The Corporate Eunuch*. New York: Crowell, 1973.

Bell, Alan P., and Martin S. Weinberg. *Homosexualities*. New York: Simon and Schuster, 1978.

Bellow, Saul. *Herzog*. London: Weidenfeld & Nicolson, 1965.

———. *Humboldt's Gift*. New York: Viking, 1973.

Belmont, David Eugene. "Early Greek Guest Friendship and Its Role in Homer's Odyssey." Ph.D. dissertation, Princeton University, 1962.

Bensman, Joseph, and Robert Lilienfeld. "Friendship and Alienation." *Psychology Today*, October 1979, pp. 56–113.

Berkinov, Louise. *Among Women*. New York: Harnon Books, 1980.

Berne, Eric. *Games People Play*. New York: Grove Press, 1964.

Block, Joel D. *Friendship: How to Give It, How to Get It*. New York: Macmillan, 1980.

Bolotin, David. *Plato's Dialogue on Friendship: An Interpretation of the Lysis, With a New Translation*. Ithaca, N.Y.: Cornell University Press, 1979.

Bradford, Ernle. *Nelson: The Essential Hero*. London: Macmillan, 1977.

* Brain, Robert. *Friends and Lovers*. New York: Basic Books, 1976.

Brenton, Myron. *Friendship*. New York: Stein & Day, 1974.

Bridges, William. *Transitions: Making Sense of Life's Changes*. Reading, Mass.: Addison-Wesley, 1981.

Bry, Adelaide. *Friendship: How to Have a Friend and Be a Friend*. New York: Grosset and Dunlap, 1979.

Buber, Martin. *I and Thou*. New York: Scribner's, 1958.

Caldwell, Mayta A., and Letitia Anne Paplau. "Sex Differences in Same Sex Friendship." Unpublished paper, University of California, Los Angeles.

* Carpenter, Edward. *Ioläus: An Anthology of Friendship*. London: Swan Sonnenschien, 1906.

Cheever, John. *Falconer*. New York: Knopf, 1977.

Cicero, Marcus Tullius. *De Amicitia*, translated by William Armistead Falconer. Cambridge: Harvard University Press, 1921.

Claremont de Castillejo, Irene. *Knowing Woman*. New York: Putnam, 1973.

Clarke, Samuel. *The Life and Death of Hannibal the Great Captain of the Carthaginians . . . As Also the Life and Death of Epaminondas, the Great Captain of the Thebans.* London: William Miller, 1665.

Collange, Christiane. *Ça va les hommes?* Paris: Grasset, 1981.

Conde Abellán, Carmen. *La amistad en la literatura española.* Madrid: Editorial Alhambra, 1944.

Couloubaritsis, Lambros. "La Philia." *Annales de l'Institut de Philosophie.* Brussels: Université Libre de Bruxelles, 1970.

———. "Le rôle du *Pathos* dans l'amitié aristotelicienne." *Diotima, 8* (1980): 175–82.

Dawley, Harold H., Jr. *Friendship: How to Make and Keep Friends.* Englewood Cliffs, N.J.: Prentice-Hall, 1980.

Degler, Carl N. *At Odds: Women and the Family in America from the Revolution to the Present Day.* Oxford: Oxford University Press, 1980.

Duck, Steven W. *Personal Relationships and Personal Constructs.* New York: John Wiley, 1973.

Dugas, Ludovic. *L'Amitié antique.* Paris: Librairie Felix Alcan, 1914.

Durkheim, Emile. *Suicide: A Study in Sociology,* translated by J. A. Spaulding and G. Simpson. New York: The Free Press, 1951.

The Epic of Gilgamesh, translated by N. K. Sandars. Harmondsworth, England: Penguin Books, 1972.

Erikson, Erik H. *Childhood and Society.* New York: Norton, 1950.

Faderman, Lilian. *Surpassing the Love of Men: Romantic Friendship and Love Between Women from the Renaissance to the Present.* New York: Morrow, 1981.

Fast, I., and J. W. Broedel. "Intimacy and Distance in the Interpersonal Relationships of Persons Prone to Depression." *Journal of Projective Techniques and Personality Assessment, 31,* no. 6 (1967): 7–12.

Fasteau, Marc Feigan. *The Male Machine.* New York: McGraw-Hill, 1975.

Firestone, Ross. *A Book of Men: Visions of the Male Experience.* New York: Stonehill, 1978.

Fischer, Claude S., and Stacey J. Oliker. *Friendship, Sex and the Life Cycle.* Berkeley: Institute of Urban and Regional Development, University of California, 1980.

Fiske, Adele M. *The Survival and Development of the Ancient Concept of Friendship in the Early Middle Ages.* Cuernavaca, Mexico: Centro Intercultural de Documentacion, 1970.

* Fraisse, Jean Claude. *Philia: La notion d'amitié dans la philosophie antique.* Paris: Libraire Philosophique J. Vrin, 1974.

Friday, Nancy. *Men in Love.* London: Arrow Books, 1980.

Friedan, Betty. *The Feminine Mystique.* New York: Dell, 1977.

Garnett, Edward, ed. *Letters from Conrad.* London: Nonesuch Press, 1927.

Gerson, Frederick. *L'Amitié au XVIIIe siècle.* Paris: La Pensée Universelle, 1974.

Goffman, Erving. *Asylums.* New York: Doubleday Anchor, 1961.

———. *Strategic Interaction.* Philadelphia: University of Pennsylvania Press, 1969.

Goldberg, Herb. *The Hazards of Being Male.* New York: Nash, 1976.

———. *The New Male.* New York: Morrow, 1979.

Gordon, Suzanne. *Lonely in America.* New York: Simon and Schuster, 1979.

Gould, Roger. *Transformations.* New York: Simon and Schuster, 1978.

Greenberg, Joel. "Relationships." *New York Times,* July 27, 1981, p. 35.

Grossman, Richard. *Choosing and Changing.* New York: Dutton, 1978.

Hearn, Janice W. *Making Friends, Keeping Friends.* New York: Doubleday, 1979.

Heller, Joseph. *Good as Gold.* London: Cape, 1979.

———. *Something Happened.* New York: Knopf, 1975.

Howard, Jane. *Families.* New York: Simon and Schuster, 1978.

Huncke, Herbert. *Huncke's Journal.* New York: The Poet's Press, 1965.

Illich, Ivan. *Toward a History of Needs.* New York: Pantheon, 1977.

James, Muriel, and Louis M. Savary. *The Heart of Friendship.* New York: Harper & Row, 1976.

Josephson, Eric, and Mary Josephson, eds. *Man Alone: Alienation in Modern Society.* New York: Dell, 1962.

Jourard, Sidney M. *The Transparent Self.* New York: Van Nostrand, 1964.

Jung, C. G. *Memories, Dreams, Reflections.* New York: Pantheon, 1963.

———. "The Stages of Life." In *The Portable Jung,* edited by Joseph Campbell. New York: Viking, 1971.

Kupffer, Elisar von. *Lieblingminne und Freundesliebe in der Weltlitteratur.* Leipzig: M. Spohr, 1905.

Lankheit, Klaus. *Das Freundschaftsbild der Romantik.* Heidelberg: C. Winter, 1952.

Lasch, Christopher. *The Culture of Narcissism: American Life in an Age of Diminishing Expectations.* New York: Norton, 1979.

———. *Haven in a Heartless World: The Family Besieged.* New York: Basic Books, 1977.

Laslett, Peter. "The World We Have Lost." In *Man Alone: Alienation in Modern Society,* edited by Eric and Mary Josephson. New York: Dell, 1962.

Leefeldt, Christine, and Ernest Callenbach. *The Art of Friendship.* New York: Pantheon, 1979.

Lefaucher, Nadine. "Qu'attendez-vous de vos amis?" *Psychologie,* May 1981, pp. 49–56.

Lepp, Ignace. *Ways of Friendship.* New York: Macmillan, 1968.

Levinson, Daniel J., et al. *The Seasons of a Man's Life.* New York: Knopf, 1978.

Lewis, C. S. *The Four Loves.* London: Geoffrey Bles, 1960.

Leyton, Elliott, ed. *The Compact: Selected Dimensions of Friendship.* St. John's, Newf.: Memorial University of Newfoundland, 1975.

Lindsey, Karen. *Friends as Family.* Boston: Beacon Press, 1981.

Lipsett, Seymour Martin, and Everett Ladd. "Anatomy of a Decade." *Public Opinion,* December–January 1980, pp. 2–9.

Longford, Elizabeth. *Wellington: Pillar of State.* London: Weidenfeld & Nicolson, 1972.

Lowenthal, Marjorie, and C. Haven. "Interaction and Adaptation: Intimacy as a Critical Variable." *American Sociological Review, 33,* no. 1 (1968): 20–30.

Lowenthal, Marjorie, and L. Weiss. "Intimacy and Crises in Adulthood." *The Counseling Psychologist, 6,* no. 1 (1976): 10–15.

Lualdi, Maria. *Il problema della philia e il Liside platonico.* Milano: Celuc, 1974.

Lucas-Dubreton, J. *La vie quotidienne au temps des Medicis.* Paris: Hachette, 1958.

Lynd, Helen Merrell. *On Shame and the Search for Identity.* New York: Harcourt, Brace & World, 1958.

McGinnis, Alan Loy. *The Friendship Factor: How to Get Closer to the People You Care For.* Minneapolis: Augsburg, 1979.

Mailer, Norman. *The Executioner's Song.* London: Hutchinson, 1979.

Marin, Peter. "The New Narcissism." *Harper's,* October 1975, pp. 45–46.

Marx, Karl. *Capital.* New York: Modern Library, 1936.

Maugham, W. Somerset. *Of Human Bondage.* London: William Heinemann, 1915.

May, Rollo. *Love and Will.* New York: Norton, 1969.

Merrill, Susan Lee. "Patterns and Functions of Close Friendship in Relation to Personal Adjustment." Ph.D. dissertation, University of Minnesota, 1974.

Michaels, Leonard. *The Men's Club.* New York: Farrar Straus Giroux, 1981.

Mills, Laurens Joseph. *One Soul in Bodies Twain: Friendship in Tudor Literature and Stuart Drama.* Bloomington, Ind.: Principia Press, 1937.

Mireaux, Emile. *La vie quotidienne au temps d'Homère.* Paris: Hachette, 1954.

Montagu, Ashley. *The Natural Superiority of Women.* New York: Macmillan, 1968.

Montaigne, Michel de. "On Friendship." In *The Complete Essays of Montaigne,* translated by Donald M. Frame. Stanford: Stanford University Press, 1965.

Morris, Willie. "Good Friends: Dogs, Sons and Others." *Parade,* September 7, 1980, pp. 7–9.

Moustakas, Clark. *Loneliness.* New York: Prentice-Hall, Spectrum Books, 1961.

Newman, Mildred, and Bernard Berkowitz. *How to Be Your Own Best Friend.* London: Pan Books, 1974.

Olsen, Kate. "The Narrowing Circles of Middle-Aged Managers." *Psychology Today,* March 1980, p. 28.

Paine, R. "Anthropological Approaches to Friendship." *Humanitas, 6,* no. 2 (1970): 139–60.

Parlee, Mary Brown, et al. "*Psychology Today*'s Survey Report on Friendship in America: The Friendship Bond." *Psychology Today,* October 1979, pp. 45–113.

Puschmann-Nalenz, Barbara. *Loves of Comfort and Despair: Konzeption von Freudschaft und Liebe in Shakespeares Sonetten.* Frankfurt: Akademische Verlagsgesellschaft, 1974.

Rasch, Wolfdietrich. *Freundschaftskult und Freundschaftsdichtung im deutschen Schrifttum.* Halle/Salle, 1936.

Rich, Adrienne. *Of Woman Born.* New York: Norton, 1976.

* Reisman, John M. *Anatomy of Friendship.* New York: Irvington Publishers, 1979.

Riesman, David. *The Lonely Crowd.* New Haven: Yale University Press, 1950.

Riveline, Maurice. *Montaigne et l'amitié.* Paris: F. Alcan, 1939.

Rubin, Lillian. *Women of a Certain Age: The Midlife Search for Self.* New York: Harper & Row, 1979.

Rubin, Michael. *Men Without Masks, Writings from the Journals of Modern Men.* Reading, Mass.: Addison-Wesley, 1980.

Rubin, Zick. "Seeking a Cure for Loneliness." *Psychology Today,* October 1979, pp. 82–90.

Rubinstein, Carin, Phillip Shaver, and Letitia Anne Peplau. "Loneliness." *Human Nature,* February 1979, pp. 58–65.

Schofield, William. *Psychotherapy: The Purchase of Friendship.* Englewood Cliffs, N. J.: Prentice-Hall, 1964.

Selden, Elizabeth S. *The Book of Friendship: An International Anthology.* Boston: Houghton Mifflin, 1947.

Seneca, Lucius Annaeus. "Quomodo amicitia continenda sit," edited by Otto Rossbach. In *De Senecae philosophi librorum recensione et emendatione,* edited by G. S. Studemund. Breslau: 1887–98.

Serrano, Miguel. *C. G. Jung and Herman Hesse: A Record of Two Friendships.* New York: Schocken Books, 1968.

Shakespeare, William. *The Two Gentlemen of Verona.* In *The Complete Signet Shakespeare,* edited by Sylvan Barnett. New York: Harcourt Brace, 1963.

Sidney, Sir Philip. *The Countesse of Pembroke's Arcadia.* In *The Prose Works of Sir Philip Sidney,* edited by Albert Feuillerat. Cambridge: Cambridge University Press, 1962.

Smith-Rosenberg, Carroll. "The Female World of Love and Ritual: Relations Between Women in Nineteenth Century America." *Signs 1,* Autumn 1975, pp. 1–29.

Snow, C. P. *The Light and the Dark.* London: Faber & Faber, 1947.

Soupault, Phillipe. *L'Amitié.* Paris: Hachette, 1965.

Steel, Ronald. "Love Letters from Olympus." *Esquire,* August 1980, pp. 50–61.

Stein, Harry. "Just Good Friends." *Esquire,* August 1980, pp. 21–23.

Sullivan, Harry Stack. *The Interpersonal Theory of Psychiatry.* New York: Norton, 1953.

Tiger, Lionel. *Men in Groups.* New York: Random House, 1969.

Tocqueville, Alexis de. *Democracy in America.* New York: Knopf, 1951.

Todd, Janet M. *Women's Friendship in Literature.* New York: Columbia University Press, 1980.

Tolson, Andrew. *The Limits of Masculinity.* New York: Harper & Row, 1977.

Tomizza, Fulvio. *L'Amicizia.* Milano: Rizzoli, 1980.

Tripp, C. A. *The Homosexual Matrix.* New York: McGraw-Hill, 1975.

Tuchman, Barbara W. *A Distant Mirror.* New York: Knopf, 1978.

Vaillant, George E. *Adaptation to Life.* Boston: Little, Brown, 1977.

Van Vlissingen, J. F. "Friendship in History." *Humanitas,* 6, no. 2 (1970): 139–60.

Weber, Max. *Economy and Society,* edited by G. Roth and C. Wittich. New York: Bedminster Press, 1968.

Weiss, Laurence J. "Intimacy: An Intervening Factor in Adaptation." Presented at the Thirtieth Annual Scientific Meeting of the Gerontological Society, San Francisco, California, November 18–22, 1977.

Weiss, Lawrence, and M. F. Lowenthal. "Life Course Perspectives on Friendship." In *Four Stages in Life,* edited by M. F. Lowenthal et al. San Francisco: Jossey-Bass, 1975.

Weiss, Robert S. *Loneliness: The Experience of Emotional and Social Isolation.* Cambridge: MIT Press, 1974.

Weller, Sheila. "Joseph Heller and Judith Viorst: Humor Can Save Your Life." *Self,* August 1979, pp. 46–50.

Zaretsky, Eli. *Capitalism, the Family and Personal Life.* New York: Harper Colophon, 1976.